SOLVING THE YEAR 2000 PROBLEM

SOLVING THE YEAR 2000 PROBLEM

Jim Keogh

AP PROFESSIONAL

AP PROFESSIONAL is a Division of Academic Press

Boston   San Diego   New York
London   Sydney   Tokyo   Toronto

AP Professional
1300 Boylston St., Chestnut Hill, MA 02167, USA
An Imprint of Academic Press
A Division of Harcourt Brace & Company
http://www.apnet.com

United Kingdom Edition published by
ACADEMIC PRESS LIMITED
24–28 Oval Road, London NW1 7DX, GB
http://www.hbuk.cc.uk/ap/

Keogh, James Edward,
        Solving the Year 2000 Problem/Jim Keogh.
            p. cm.
        ISBN 0-12-575560-0 (alk. paper)
        1. Software maintenance. 2. Year 2000 date coversion (Computer
Systems) 1. Title
QA76.76.S64K46   1997
005.1'6—dc21   96-40429
                                                                                CIP

Printed in the United States of America

97   98   99   00   IP   9   8   7   6   5   4   3

This book is dedicated to Anne, Sandra, and Joanne,
without whose help this book could not have been possible.

Contents

The Day the Computers Go Bang

"Ten, nine, eight,...," eyes are fixed on the red apple as it is lowered down the pole. The bash of the century is under way. And with a roar that has not been heard in Times Square for 10 decades, hundreds of millions welcome in a new millennium in a celebration few will forget. Everyone will remember this night and never forget where they were when the year 2000 arrived.

It's hard to believe that we will be around for the birth of the new century in a few years. Just yesterday, it seems, Walter Cronkite's voice came into our homes across the country introducing everyone to the marvels of the times on his show *20ᵗʰ Century*. Now with the twenty-first century around the corner, those new contraptions he spoke about seem primitive by today's standards.

The marvels of the twentieth century seem endless: the automobile, the airplane, television, motion pictures, the telephone, the electric light, space travel. That particular 36,500 days of hard work and ingenuity revolutionized every aspect of our life. And, of course, computers. These gray boxes containing who knows what streamlined the storage and flow of information to a point where there's so much information computers are needed to query other computers to find the information that is needed.

One of my favorite *Twilight Zone* episodes took a frightening look at how dependent we have become on computers. Jack Klugman (before *the Odd Couple*) joined a firm as a computer engineer. He walked into this manufacturing-plant-size building and was greeted by a secretary who escorted him to the manager of the firm. The building was quiet and cool. You could hear a pin drop. Klugman sat behind the computer console, and with a startling expression looked up at the manager and asked, "Where's everyone?"

As the camera panned out showing a warehouse floor filled with an assortment of IBM computer equipment, the manager purposely remarked, "We have only three employees. My secretary, you, and myself. We don't need anyone else. The computers do all the work."

This was back in the 1960s, before Steve, Bill, and the gang got into the act, when only the largest corporations could afford computer power. The *Twilight Zone* writers were not too far off in their predictions of the future. Computers replaced millions of clerical positions along with some in the managerial ranks.

But something implied in the show materialized in force: our over dependency on computers. Have you ever stopped to think of how much we need computers? Unless you have been scoffed at by a wayward computer sending you unwarranted notices and spent days trying to talk a human into correcting the error, you probably, like most of us, have taken the benefits of computers for granted.

Ask yourself:

- Who flies your airplane?
- Who writes your paycheck?
- Who keeps track of how much money you have in the bank?
- Who tells you the price of groceries at the checkout counter?

- Who runs the videotape of your favorite show at the broadcast studio?
- Who connects your phone call?
- Who reminds you that your driver's license needs renewal?
- Who audits your tax return?
- Answer: a computer.

Shocking, isn't it? We are only needed to develop business rules, write instructions for computers to follow, and handle those rare occasions when computers make errors.

The Personal Touch

Our very social, economical, and physical lives are practically controlled by computers. Hard to believe, but consider the impact if information about you, stored in umpteen, unseen computers is inaccurate. Most of us do not realize how much information about us is kept electronically, nor the disruption to our lives if the data does not truly represent a picture of ourselves.

Begin with your birth, the record of which is registered in a governmental computer in the town where your were born—or is it? Have you checked recently? Probably not. Most of us go to Mom for a copy of our birth certificate. However, if there is a computer foul-up, you may not have been born—at least legally.

Without a birth certificate, chances are you are unable to apply for a driver's license, a passport so you can travel abroad, or be granted a Social Security card by the federal government. There is a rippling effect. Your job opportunities are slim if you do not have a valid Social Security card, and an absence of employment leaves you in a financial bind.

With little or no financial resources you will soon find yourself destitute. There is no money for rent, food, or clothes. And you have trouble applying for public assistance. You are unable to prove that you are legally entitled to welfare programs—you are not "in" any governmental computer! You don't exist! A dreadful thought—just because of one computer error.

Say that you already possess a driver's license and you have a Social Security card and a good job. What a secure feeling knowing the black picture I just painted is just a frightening thought that could not affect you. You are secure—or are you?

For many of us, money in the bank is our ace in the hole to fend off any bleak condition that can spoil our pleasant lives. We can always withdraw cash to make purchases and write checks to transfer money to pay our creditors. With luck there's a little money left over for unseen emergencies.

Do you have money in the bank? Not really. You have a dollar amount stored in your bank's computer alongside your Social Security number. The bank's computer changes this number whenever you deposit or withdraw money. Suppose that the computer comes down with a serious case of the computer flu—a virus—that wipes out your Social Security number or the dollar amount, or both. How much money will you have in the bank? Nothing.

Your bank probably has a backup of customer data and can restore the previous day's balances—restoring your "money"—if the information on the backup is intact and unaffected by the virus. And your latest bank statement is proof that your account had funds—assuming that you did not toss the statement in the garbage. However, how much time has to pass before your bank reinstates your account? Time that can be measured in months. In the meantime the money you need to pay your bills does not exist. Another dreadful thought.

The Achilles' Heel of Business

Our personal dependency on computer power is dwarfed by the greater need of industry. The lifeblood of practically every business—and the world's economy—flows through thousands of computers joined by cables, microwave transmitters, and satellites.

There is virtually no money in business except for your local sandwich shop. Businesses have not exchanged cash in decades. All the transactions are made by exchanging computer data. Just as with our funds, money owned by a corporation is really a dollar value stored in computers alongside the business's tax identification number, the equivalent to our Social Security number.

Even the simplest business transaction does not involve cash. Take the Widget Corporation. The firm orders office supplies from the NOS Corporation. The order is placed by telephone then entered into the NOS Corporation's computer. The computer sends the order to the warehouse for picking, packing, and shipping. An invoice is generated by the computer and sent to the Widget Corporation. The NOS Corporation's computer records the sale as money to be received by the firm.

If the Widget Corporation does not pay within a reasonable time period, the NOS Corporation's computer automatically creates a reminder letter which is sent. When the Widget Corporation pays, it does so by check. The check is endorsed and given to the firm's bank for electronic collection. This entire process amounts to adjusting numbers stored in four computers.

The Widget Corporation's bank account is debited the amount of the check and the NOS Corporation's bank account is credited with the same amount. Both banks electronically notify their clients of the adjustments which are automatically reflected on the books and records of both firms—on their computers.

Where is the money? There isn't any money. In business, money as we know it is a figment of our imagination. It doesn't exist primarily because of a concept called a book-entry system. A *book-entry system* is a method businesses use to limit—and in some cases eliminate—the need to use cash to complete transactions. Instead of cash, each business adjusts its books and records to reflect the movement of money between businesses.

So when a business reports that it has cash assets of $100 million, the business is really saying that alongside the firm's tax identification number there is a number of 100 million—in the computer. Chances are that the president of the firm would create a panic with the firm's bank if he asked to see the $100 million in cash. This is because the bank probably does not have the $100 million on hand to show the president of the firm. The bank's money is also a number stored in a computer alongside the bank's tax identification number.

As long as computers continue to operate, businesses do not need real money. They only need the impression of money that appears on the computer screen and on reports generated by computers.

Behind the Scenes

We gave all this power to computers for the sake of efficiency. Computers do not get tired of repeating the same mundane task and they never make errors once the correct instructions are written for the computer to follow. Computers do not ask for time off and never ask for a pay raise.

A side benefit is that computers do not dip into the till for a share of the firm's money. Computers just do what they are told to do and the person who gives those instructions is a programmer. A *programmer* interprets rules that govern the operation of a business into sometimes cryptic sentences that clearly direct the computer through a complex task—like reminding you that your credit card bill is overdue.

Anyone who has not been privy to how computers do what they do might be awed by the entire process. Somehow these super whiz kid geniuses sift through mountains of technical jargon and magically make this inanimate object come alive.

Magic? Not really. Geniuses? Not true, although some who think of themselves as such may differ with me. The entire process involves a basic understanding of common sense. Computers do what they are told to do by humans—only computers do it faster and accurately every time. If you can list the steps necessary to carry out a task in the order in which those steps are to be executed, with a little technical training, you can become a programmer.

Let's say you want a person to enter her name into your computer program. This is a very common task found in many programs. Here are the steps that are needed to perform the task:

1. Clear the screen.

2. Display a message on the screen: "Enter your name:"

3. Read whatever the person types into the keyboard.

These are the business rules—admittedly a bit sparse—that a programmer translates into instructions the computer understands. A real program, such as those used to keep track of your bank balance, is organized the same way as this small example, only there are thousands of instructions the computer must execute.

Computers do not make mistakes. Programmers who write the instructions that computers follow and those who write the business rules that programmers follow make mistakes. And those mistakes are blindly followed by the computer—over and over again with the accuracy of a computer!

The Mother of All Computer Bugs

As you enjoy the bash on New Year's Eve, many business leaders and computer professionals will look toward the sky praying that the mother of all computer failures doesn't occur at the stroke of midnight. Chances are there will be a massive computer failure that has never been seen before.

When the apple completes its journey and revelers pop open champagne to welcome in the twenty-first century, all of the computers will change the date stored inside the computer. That date is the one that programs use to perform date-sensitive tasks such as knowing when pay day arrives.

January 1, 2000, will be the date—or will it? Will the date change from 12-31-99 to 01-01-00? Whoops! What happened to the century digits in the date? Welcome to the mother of all computer bugs. Unfortunately, many computers and many computer programs only use the two-year digits and not the two century digits in the date. The "19" in the year is dropped. All years are assumed to be in the twentieth Century.

Who cares if the 19 is missing from the date? With a little common sense, anyone knows the computer means the twenty-first century and not the twentieth century. We may realize this fact, but computer programs will not because a date to a computer program is a number. And computers don't think, they just follow directions.

Here is a simple example to illustrate this point. Let's say that you want to write a program that asks a person's birth year, then calculates the person's age. Here are the business rules for this program:

- Clear the screen.

- Display a message: "Enter your birth year (i.e. 80):"

- Read the birth year from the keyboard.

- Read the current year from the software inside the computer. (This year is 97 and the year entered at the keyboard is 80.)

- Subtract the year read from the keyboard from the current year. (97 minus 80)

- Display the difference on the screen: (17).

This is a very simple program that performs basic math. Now turn the clock ahead to the year 2000 and perform the same math. The computer is told to subtract 80 from 00 (00 minus 80). Whoops! A negative 80 is the result. Yes, there is a bug in the computer program.

Who could be so dumb as to create a computer that only uses two digits instead of four digits to represent a year? How could anyone be so shortsighted not to foresee the disaster this flaw causes at the turn of the century?

The answer to the first question is most programmers and virtually all hardware manufacturers. This means there is a very strong possibility that this bug is in every program that uses a year in a calculation. That is, the millions of lines of instructions running daily on millions of computers—both big and small. And at the stroke of midnight this bug makes a very lasting appearance.

The answer to the second question is to save time and money.

Why the Problem Occurred

The problems a simple exclusion of two digits can cause are amazing. By removing the first two digits of the year, hundreds of thousands of computer programs that keep our economy stable are on the verge of a meltdown.

Is this the plot of a sinister terrorist organization? Maybe the problem is caused by a virus that some college computer whiz invented to show the world that he or she is smarter than everyone else. Or could the problem stem from actions of a rebel employee of a computer software manufacturer?

The truth is that none of these dramatic clandestine actions is the root of the mother of all bugs that infects computers throughout the world. The problem stems from a lack of foresight by computer programmers and business managers in the 1960s through the 1990s.

Programmers must develop software applications that are economical to write and to run, and development must occur quickly. When a business manager finds a need to automate a process such as with the books and records of a business, she wants the automation in place today at a reasonable cost.

Managers of application development areas of corporations attempt to comply with the framework established by the business manager which, sometimes forces the programming staff to cut corners. One such corner that was trimmed is the number of digits that represents a year. That happened back when bytes were precious. Using two digits rather than four saved space and time.

The question you are probably asking yourself is how much time and money can be saved by using only the last two digits in a year? The answer to this question requires a little diversion into the bowels of a typical computer application.

Let's begin this tour with information that is stored and used inside your computer by your computer programs. Information such as the date 1997 must be stored somewhere in your computer. This space inside your computer is called *memory*, a temporary storage facility that gets rid of the information when the computer is turned off. Another storage facility is a *disk* where information can remain intact forever.

In today's technology both computer memory and disk space are inexpensive. For a few hundred dollars practically any computer can have more memory and disk space than can be used in a year. However, back in the 1960s through the 1980s both memory and disk space were at a premium.

Information is stored as a binary value in memory. These are the familiar 1's and 0's, each of which is stored in a switch in an integrated circuit inside the computer. In the 1960s, an integrated circuit held 10 switches. By the 1970s the same size integrated circuit held 1000 switches. Today an integrated circuit holds 100 million switches.

Likewise, a microprocessor in the 1970s addressed 64,000 bytes of memory (a byte uses eight switches). By the 1990s, a microprocessor addresses four gigabytes of memory. Processing speeds of information increased from 300,000 instructions per second (0.3 MIPS) to 20 million instructions per second (20 MIPS) during the same time period.

Programmers were instructed to economize on the use of memory and disk space, so each piece of information was looked at carefully. Programmers asked themselves and the business manager if the information was required to perform the necessary task. If so, they then needed to know how much of the information was necessary for the program to perform the task.

A programmer could reduce the size of the year information from four to two characters. This made available spaces to hold two other characters of information in memory and on the disk. Although two characters does not seem to be much, it is substantial.

This technique not only occurred with application programs such as an accounting system, but it was also used in the operating system, microcode found in computer chips, and even in the logic etched into the chip.

Information is typically stored with other related information both in memory and on disk. Computer programmers call this information a *record*. For example, your name, address, telephone, and the date that you were hired is one record in your company's personnel system.

Let's say that your company has a million employees. This means that there are one million records in the company's personnel system. When the programmer chopped off the first two digits of the year, she made available space for two million characters.

Imagine the space that suddenly became available for other information when the programmer trimmed the century digits from every place in the company's database that had date information. This was a great coup for the programmer who discovered this technique for economizing expensive computer resources.

The century was trimmed from the date for another reason—convenience. Think for a moment. When you enter information into a computer, you notice that some of the information is already displayed on the screen. For example, today's date probably appears on the form without you having to enter it from the keyboard. This is because the programmer used the date found inside your computer as the date for the form.

Sometimes, however, this date (called the system's date) is inaccurate. Therefore, the programmer must allow you to correct the date on the screen. Some programmers try to make this task even easier by allowing you to change only the two year digits. The programmers assumed the two century digits would never change. We now know they made a wrong assumption.

Efficiency and convenience are two of the major reasons why every computer manager in the world is now faced with the almost insurmountable task of inserting the two century digits back into the year data.

Business managers and programmers knew dropping the century digits was short-sighted planning. They knew this solution was only a temporary fix and that someday at the turn of the century someone was going to feel the effects of this lack of long-range planning. But by then those business managers and programmers who made the original decision would be retired. The problem would not be theirs to solve.

Then there is the problem of the tool that many programmers used decades ago to build their programs. The tool is the old COBOL compiler that IBM provided to their customers to build application programs.

A programmer writes a program using English-like words, which are then translated into instructions that the computer understands. A compiler, which itself is a program, handles this translation. The only problem is that the COBOL compilers decades ago use two digits to represent a year and not four digits. So even if programmers foresaw the problem, they could do little to avoid it because of the compiler. COBOL is by no means the only culprit. The thinking was that surely these programs would be replaced by the year 2000. IBM built two-digit dates into the CMOS on their IBM PCs. In fact, they *just* stopped.

Even when the hardware and software tools were capable of using four-digit years, programmers and software and hardware manufacturers kept repeating the same mistake. The style of representing a year as two digits became the standard without much thought given to the impact this error would have on the future execution of the program.

Each year managers, who recognized that this problem exists, had to assess the life span of the system compared with the time and cost of fixing the year 2000 problem. Most managers decided not to fix the system, hoping that someone would build a new system long before the problem affected the firm (or until the system was no longer their responsibility). After all, if you might change your system anyway, why go ahead and fix the problem now?

Some financial firms began addressing this problem in the 1970s since some of their systems performed date calculations that extended into the twenty-first century. However, most firms did not realize the potential impact of the year 2000 problem until recently.

Not an Easy Fix

Now that you have an appreciation for the seriousness of the problem, you are probably wondering why all the big fuss. Why are business leaders and computer professionals so concerned about inserting the missing two digits into the year?

The task of inserting the missing two digits into a year is not very complicated for most programs. However, the problem is to determine where these corrections need to be made. Where are the problem lines of code?

To understand the depth of this problem, we will divert a little and show you the realities of how a computer department functions. The focus of many computer departments—business and government alike—is to develop new application programs.

Once an application is introduced, ("placed in production"), attention is refocused on another new application. That is, the programmers and program managers who built the application move on to another new application.

Any changes to an existing application are made by other programmers. The old saying "If it isn't broken, don't fix it" applies to computer programs. Few programmers look forward to the assignment of modifying a program that runs perfectly well in production. The reason for this cowardliness is that no programmer wants to be blamed for breaking a mission critical program.

So programmers who receive such assignments avoid touching the instructions in the existing program. Instead, they build programs separately from the production program, then hook these programs into the production program. A *hook* means that only one instruction is added to the production program and that instruction calls the new separate program.

Most large corporations stay in business thanks to old, reliable production programs that have been running for decades. These are called *legacy systems*. And since they have been functioning flawlessly for so long there is a good chance there are hundreds of other programs that have been hooked into the production program. These are those separate programs that modified the original functionality of the production program.

Of course, most firms experience a turnover of their programming staff every five years or less. This means that the programmers who wrote the original program and those programmers who wrote modifications to those programs are nowhere to be found.

This leaves many organizations with very large, mission critical legacy programs that work fine but there is no one on the firm's computer staff who knows every facet of the program. In very basic terms, no one knows where all the instructions are that tell the computer to perform date calculations.

Where Is the Source Code?

Reading the previous section leaves you with a frightening impression. Business managers assume that the firm's computer whiz kids have everything under control. In reality, most computer professionals work in survival mode.

If you become responsible for a production program that works fine, then you will avoid any request to change the program. Always counter such requests with a proposal to build a new program. And if that does not satisfy the business manager, then build the required modification as a side program that is hooked into the production program. Put simply, do as little as necessary.

This attitude is not exclusive of computer personnel. Many business managers have the same philosophy. Avoid being blamed for something that does not work since it is not healthy for your career.

However, the problem with inserting two more digits to represent the date is further compounded by the lack of administrative skills prevalent in many computer departments. There is an excellent chance that no one knows where the source code is for the firm's legacy systems.

Source code is the term used to describe the English-like instructions that are written by a programmer to tell the computer what to do. The source code is then translated into an executable program by a program called a *compiler*.

How could a computer department of a large corporation misplace the source code of critical programs? The answer is: very easily.

Responsibility for old legacy programs is passed down to programmers who are told many times not to worry about the programs. This is especially true if the program has operated perfectly for years and no one ever requires modification of the program.

"Don't worry about it. The program runs fine. No one has asked for changes to the program in years." This is the common phrase heard when responsibility for a legacy program is turned over to another programmer. The programmer is responsible for the program—on paper. In reality, no one knows much about the program including the location of the source code.

The Problems of Correcting the Date

The first problem programmers face in trying to fix the date is locating all the places in all the programs where the year is referenced by two digits instead of four digits. It has been reported in the press that one major insurance company faces the task of correcting 120 million instructions in hundreds of millions of instructions that are running in mission critical programs.

Assuming the source code for these programs is found, teams of programmers must scan through each line of source code looking for instructions that tell the computer a year of 00 means 1900. Once found, the corrections can be made to the instruction.

If programmers are fortunate, they can use a tool to perform electronic searches of source code looking for keywords that could be used to refer to a date or year (more about tools later in this chapter and in a later chapter of this book). This assumes that the programmer who wrote the original program used common keywords to represent a date and year. Otherwise, scanning the file electronically is useless. And most computer departments rarely enforce standard naming conventions for dates used in programs.

Now what happens if the source code cannot be found? Another tool must be used to disassemble the executable file back into source code. If this process is successful, then programmers begin scanning the source code. However, if the disassembly process fails, then there is no source code to scan.

In such a case, programmers must test the executable program to determine if it is affected by the two-digit date problem. If those tests prove a problem exists, then programmers and business managers must seriously consider recreating the program from scratch.

Let us be optimistic for a moment. The source code is available and corrected by the programmers. The source code must be translated into an executable file that the computer understands. The translation is performed by a compiler. However, some older COBOL compilers do not allow years to be represented in four digits. This means that the updated source code will not be successfully translated into the language the computer can read.

The next step is for the programmers to purchase a new compiler, one that accepts a four-digit date. As expected, there could be other incompatibilities between the old source code and the new compiler. Now all the source code files must be recompiled using the new compiler and be thoroughly tested. There could be instructions in the old source code that cannot be interpreted by the new compiler.

Even if the compiler does not have to be updated, the source code must be thoroughly tested with the other programs that run on the company's computers to determine if the changes adversely affect the operation of other programs.

Stop and ask yourself: Does your company have the programming staff to perform all these tasks before New Year's Eve, 1999?

No Room on the Screen or in the Database

The problem with the missing two digits in the date seems to affect only programs that perform date calculations. However, there is still the problem about space: space on the screen and space in the database.

Let us begin with a look at the problem of space on the screen. Programmers carefully plan how information is laid out on the screen. Programmers incorporate the logical flow of information as well as the logical flow of entering data on a screen into every screen displayed by a program.

A question that must be answered is this: Is there enough room on the screen to display two additional digits to represent the year? If there is room, then no problem exists. However, if there is not sufficient room on the screen, then the programmer must redesign the screen, which could impact how the screen is used by the business unit.

The next potential problem has to do with space availability in the database.

Some databases might have reached the limit on the number of pieces of information that can be stored in the database. This happens because over time legacy programs and associated databases grow in size. And the database management tool used to organize the information is technology that was new in the 1960s through 1980s and has built-in limitations that are not found in technology used today.

This could mean the entire structure of the database needs to be redesigned, which could require additional changes in the source code of programs that use the information stored in the database. Alternatively, more room may need to be built into the database.

Everyone's Problem

The mother of all bugs is not isolated to your firm or industry. Everyone is affected by it. And the repercussions of this problem are even more dramatic than the rippling effect I described so far in this chapter.

Let us say that the date problem has had minimal effect on your firm. There were a few programs that had the missing digits and your staff repaired the damage in time. The cost of the repair was an acceptable business expense and didn't affect the bottom line numbers too much. So your firm is on solid footing for the year 2000—or is it?

On New Year's Eve you will be one of those carefree managers who dances in the twenty-first century—or can you be carefree? You may join those who look to the sky and pray that their programs will not come crashing down at the stroke of midnight.

For most medium- and large-size corporations, transactions are conducted via computers. Money is transferred electronically to another firm's bank account. Banks send daily status reports on balances to the firm's computer for reconciliation. In many industries, orders for supplies and inventory are sent electronically.

No computer is really isolated in business today. Computers talk to other computers and exchange information critical to each firm's business operations.

So it is safe to say that your firm may fix the digit problem on your computers, but for everything to work smoothly on the first business day of the new century the problem must be fixed on all the computers that are used to communicate information to other computers.

Can your business continue operating if computers of key business partners are not working properly? This question must be answered by every business manager before he or she can pop the cork and welcome in the new century.

Your Staff Jumping Ship

As your programmers are isolating and fixing the lines of instructions in your programs to correct this problem, keep in mind that these people are technicians who have little stake in your company and can quickly move to a job in a different firm.

Older programmers who might have helped to cause the problem in the first place might also be moving toward the door; first to avoid repercussions from management when fingers begin to point, then to move on to potentially better paying jobs. Their old programming skills are back in demand.

There are not many programmers who specialize in fixing the year 2000 bug. To this point, they do not teach this repair in colleges nor in technical schools. Programmers learn by the seat of their pants and at their employer's expense.

This means that you are giving your programmers a very marketable skill that is needed by every computer department. Once your first program is fixed, those programmers who worked on the project have acquired this new skill. They have informally graduated from the Year 2000 Bug Fixing School.

The question is will these programmers remain with your firm to fix the rest of your programs or will they jump ship and move to a firm paying more money? Furthermore, can you afford to risk losing these programmers? They are in short supply.

There is no easy answer to these questions. Business managers need to weigh the factors, make a decision, and hope it is the correct one.

Is Your Company Affected by This Problem?

Does your firm have any computer systems that are date sensitive? Most companies have such a system and probably 30 or 40 of them which are critical to the mission of the company. So, if your firm is like most companies, your systems have the year 2000 bug.

Just think of a simple mortgage calculation that is performed hundreds of thousands of times a day by computer systems in the banking industry. Say the system needs to calculate the repayment of a 20-year mortgage taken out in 1997. The first two years work fine in the calculation, but then the century changes and the year changes from 99 to 00. Chances are that the system is unable to perform the calculation.

Even if your systems do not perform date calculations, they are still affected by the bug. The problem exists at all levels of programs, from application programs to the microcode in the BIOS in your personal computer. The BIOS is embedded on a computer chip in your personal computer.

Unless you have purchased a computer recently, your old reliable computer may be attacked by the year 2000 bug—and there is little you can do about it—especially if the bug is embedded inside a critical chip on your computer's circuit board.

And if you think that your systems are not date sensitive, think again. Your company's bills are paid by your computer systems based on the system date on the chip inside your computer. If you are using the wrong date and the bills do not get paid on time, your company may accrue interest charges and your company's credit rating could be affected.

Furthermore, some firms like utility companies and credit card companies stop providing services if bills are not paid on time. You could find yourself turning the lights on in the office one morning in the next century only to find out you are still in the dark.

Or you could entertain a large, potential client only to find out when you receive the check that your credit card was canceled. Your company's computer failed to pay the corporate credit card bill on time.

What is worse is that your company's operations could be affected by this problem today! Although the year 2000 is a short distance into the future, some of your systems use dates in the future as part of their processing.

Misconceptions

Some managers see the year 2000 problem as one that is only associated with hardware—those little chips inside your computer. The solution to the problem is easy, but expensive: Replace a few circuit boards inside your computers and the problem goes away.

Sorry, this is not the answer. The problem is not with the hardware but with the software. Chips inside your computer that are affected by the problem are encoded with small pieces of code called *microcode*. These are instructions a programmer entered into a computer which were then electronically encoded onto the chip.

When the programmer decided to use only a two-digit year in the microcode, the programmer infected the chip—and your computer— with a software bug, not a hardware bug. A software bug that is best solved by replacing the chip.

But this is just part of the problem. Software throughout your computer—those your firm built and those purchased—probably uses only a two-digit-year. So even if you changed the chip inside your computer to read a four-digit-year, most of your programs are still using only the year component of the date, not the century.

Another misconception is that the problem only exists with application programs. Those are the software programs that run your payroll and keep you in business. Actually, those microcode programs encoded into chips are used in a lot of devices that you do not usually consider to be a "computer." These include elevators, automobiles, and VCRs. Even some refrigerators have microcoded chips. And the list goes on almost endlessly. Nearly everything you can think of is computerized in some way. Are these devices date sensitive? Will they stop working at the turn of the century? There is no way to give a general answer. You must investigate each device yourself—before the stroke of midnight December 31, 1999.

There is one last misconception that should be set straight. The year 2000 bug does not exist only on mainframe computer systems. Nor does the bug reside only on legacy systems. This is an easy misconception to develop since most of the press talks about the hidden trouble inside mainframe, legacy systems.

In fact, the year 2000 problem is in over-the-counter desktop programs that have been sold in recent years.

There Are No Quick Fixes

Addressing the year 2000 problem in your company takes on the magnitude of a mission to the moon for NASA. Earlier in this chapter you learned about the real problems that face your technicians when trying to rectify the condition.

The actual repair of the problem in most cases is not difficult at all. In fact, a programmer fresh out of college should be able to make the necessary change in the code, assuming that he or she knows the necessary programming languages. (Later in this book you will see how to make these code changes.) The problem is finding out where those changes are to be made in your systems.

Think of all the systems that run your company. Does anyone really know how many there are? Probably not. Does anyone know where the source code is for all those programs? Probably not. Then how is a programmer going to correct the year 2000 bug?

Companies have spent nearly a half a year trying to identify—not fix—all their systems, source code, and store-bought software programs that keep their company operational. This does not include the time necessary to assess each system to determine if the system is affected by the problem.

All that work plus the repair job, testing, and implementing the changes lie ahead of you. And the clock keeps ticking closer to a deadline that cannot be moved back—a deadline after which the systems might stop working altogether.

And of course there is the expense of all this work. Published reports project cost for a midsize company to be slightly over $5 million. This is money that is above and beyond current operating expense and money that may not be in the current budget.

....

What Needs To Be Done

The process of fixing the problem begins with a proper plan of attack. You must consider all aspects of the problem, not only finding where to insert the century digits. The ramifications of the year 2000 problem are so immense that you require a team of people with diverse skills to tackle the problem.

The team, called the year 2000 team in many companies, must be comprised of business and technical managers, financial officers, and attorneys, each of whom has the ability to analyze the problem based on their specialty knowledge and to make recommendations to the team. Furthermore, the team must have the full power to make decisions and enact policies directly.

Support staff reporting to the team must identify all the systems—including elevators and building security devices—that could be affected by the year 2000 problem. This inventory must be well documented using any number of techniques including one described in detail later in this book.

The inventory serves as the focal point for the team to conduct a high-level review of each system. The team must determine a number of factors, including whether or not the company has the legal right to examine the code of the system and if the company has the legal right to fix the year 2000 bug.

As you will read in later chapters, software acquired by your company from a vendor is not owned by your company. Instead, your company purchases the right to use the software under the terms of the licensing agreement with the vendor. Normally, the licensing agreement does not give you permission to examine the source code nor change the source code. More about this later.

The team also must determine the impact a system has on the operations of the company. For each system, the team must ask: Is this system mission critical? Those that are, must be assigned a high priority and moved to the top of the list of systems that must undergo a detailed analysis by the technical staff.

Another high-level decision for the team to make is whether or not all of the pieces are available to be reviewed and, if necessary, fixed. The executable copy of a legacy system is always found during the inventory process because this is the program that runs every day. However, the corresponding source code is sometimes not found during the inventory process. In this case, the team must decide how to approach this problem. One solution is to disassemble the executable copy of the program - if the staff has the tools and know-how to perform this task.

But before you even raise this question, the team must know if the company has the legal right to disassemble the program. This is not necessarily an easy question to answer especially when a legacy system is involved. There may be no records that indicate whether or not the company owns the system outright.

Another solution is for the team to have the system reverse engineered. This is a technical and legal technique whereby a company's technical staff replicates the functionality of the system without looking at the system's source code. A complete discussion of how to use this technique is presented later in this book.

If the source code is available, however, the team's next step is to order an evaluation of the complete system. This must include all the databases that are used by the system, all files that input data into the system, and files that are generated by the system.

This assessment is made by the technical staff who must sift through the source code looking for places where dates are used for calculations and manipulation. Likewise, they must review date fields in databases associated with the system to determine if the date fields need to be adjusted and if there is room in the database to insert the two century digits in each date field.

Fortunately, there are tools available that can make this process speedier than if programmers had to manually look at each of the thousands of lines of code that make up the system.

The results of this review provide the team with a scope of the impact of the year 2000 problem on each system. The team will know:

- The general condition of the code;
- The number of places in the code that need changing;
- Date fields that need to be modified; and
- Potential problems with input and output files.

Other factors can be considered in the assessment process which are covered in detail in a later chapter.

The team must then decide on the level of effort necessary to make the system year 2000 compliant. The team must consider many points when reviewing the results of the assessment of each system. They must know:

- How much time is necessary to fix the system and associated databases;
- What technical skills are necessary to make these repairs;
- What resources need to be used; and
- How much the repair will cost the company.

Notice that these are high-level factors that are considered by the team, factors that help the team decide whether to move ahead and repair the system or to rebuild the system, (which in some cases is the more cost-effective and least time-consuming choice).

As you can imagine, this investigative process is very time consuming and in many cases it can take up to six months of a full-time effort to arrive at a full assessment of the impact the year 2000 bug has on the systems of the company.

Still More Planning

The first phase of the team's efforts results in having a full understanding of the problem. This is sufficient information to move to the next phase, which is the creation of a full work plan for the year 2000 project. A *work plan* specifies:

- The order in which the systems will be repaired;
- Staff assignments;
- Resource allocations, and
- Financing.

Simply said, the work plan tells everyone:

- Which system is going to be fixed;
- When the system is going to be fixed;
- How the system is going to be fixed; and
- Who will fix it.

This is the stage when formal plans are placed on paper in the form of leveling diagrams and a Gannt chart, and the critical path is defined. *Leveling diagrams* help divide the year 2000 project into big pieces. Each big piece is a system. Each system is then divided into medium pieces such as programs and databases. Each medium piece is further reduced into smaller pieces such as routines within programs and tables within databases.

The leveling diagram graphically illustrates the relationships among all the big pieces and the relationship among a big piece and the associated medium and small pieces.

The *Gannt chart* uses a bar-graph-like illustration to show milestones of the project and all the tasks that are necessary to complete each milestone. Each task is related to other tasks to show dependencies of tasks. A block of time is indicated on the chart indicating when work on the task begins and ends.

Resources such as staffing and computer equipment are also associated with each task. This enables managers to account properly for each task that must be completed to make a system or all the systems compliant by the year 2000.

A feature of a Gannt chart is the ability to draw the critical path of the project. The *critical path* is a listing of tasks that must be completed sequentially for a milestone to be reached. If one task falls behind the planned completion date, then all the dependent tasks that follow will also fall behind, making the entire project fall behind schedule.

Gannt charts and the critical path are produced by project management software such as Microsoft Project. You will find a complete discussion on how to use these project planning techniques later in this book.

The team must insist on using such techniques even in the face of opposition from the firm's systems department. Corporate systems departments use such techniques infrequently during the development of a typical system. However, no systems department has ever revised all their systems at the same time. Furthermore, no systems department has ever had a project deadline that could not be moved.

The only way the systems department is going to successfully renovate all the systems by the real-life, drop-dead, immovable deadline is by using formal planning tools.

Now to the Fix

There are four common ways to fix your systems to make them year 2000 compliant:

1. Expand the date digits to include the century digits in your databases.

2. Encode your programs to account for the century digits during calculations and date manipulations.

3. Create a sliding window that makes assumptions about the century based on the current year.

4. Twiddle with bits to squeeze four digits into the current number of bytes that are used to represent two digits.

All of these techniques are discussed in greater detail later in this book, however, let us take a glimpse at what is to come.

Expanding the date field in your databases is an obvious choice. This explicitly specifies the century and always remains in the database. There is no opportunity for confusion.

However, there may be no room in some older databases to add the additional digits. Furthermore, programs still might need to be changed, especially those that extract the year from the date data. Such a program looks for a two-digit year while the data contains a four-digit year, and there is the problem of the layouts of printed reports and data displayed on the screen. These forms are designed for a two-digit year; now there are two more digits and there may not be room on the form to hold the data.

The sliding window technique is a fast and easy way to fix the problem as long as the date data are within 100 years. First, a 100-year range is selected such as 1980 through 2079. Two-digit years that are greater than 79 are assumed to be in the 20th century, and two-digit years that are less than 80 are assumed to be in the twenty-first century.

Each year the window slides forward a year. This technique is fine for systems that do not require dates that span more than 100 years. Those that do require date manipulation beyond this range cannot be fixed using this method.

Bit twiddling involves tinkering with the way the year is represented in the field. The year 1996 is presented as 07CC in hexadecimal and the year 2000 is presented as 07D0. Both of these values used the same number of bytes as the two-digit date.

Bit twiddling is an explicit and permanent way to fix the date. However, since the form of a twiddled bit is not in a format expected by most programs, every program that accesses the bit twiddled date must convert the date back to the original format before the date can be used by the program.

Later in this book we will look closely at these plans and review guidelines to help you decide which method or combination of methods is the best solution for fixing each of your systems.

The Toolbox

If someone told you that you must read each line of the million lines of code that make up your systems to find just those lines that use dates, you would probably go crazy. However, this is the task your year 2000 team is telling your technical staff to perform.

Fortunately, there are tools your technicians can use to transform this laborious job into manageable tasks. There are tools that can assist everyone associated with the project to do the job more efficiently. Later in this book we will review the more popular tools that are available on the market. For now, we merely survey these tools.

Tools can be divided into these general categories:

- Project management;
- Code restructuring and editing;
- Code generation; and
- System testing.

Project management software is used to schedule and track each task that must be performed to fix a system. It is also used to help manage resources needed during the repair process.

These tools help management to analyze the complexity of the job, to estimate the size of the project, and to determine the resources necessary to get the job done on time.

Although the thought of project management tools brings to mind Gantt charts and leveling diagrams, these tools can do more to help you with the project. You can use these tools to show automatically the flow of data throughout the system and how programs call other programs and routines. The output of these tools clearly shows all the data used by each program of your system. You may find systems that are no longer necessary at this stage.

Furthermore, some project management tools enable your technicians to slice into a system level by level beginning with a high-level overview of the system, then moving lower into each program and routine. This process continues into the logic of each program.

The nearly insurmountable problem of searching through a million lines of code does not seem so difficult when you use project management tools. These tools do all the sifting and report to you the results. You need only analyze the results to determine what code, if any, needs to be fixed.

Then once your technician has an idea of which lines of codes need repairs, she can use one or more code restructuring and editing tools.

Code restructuring and editing tools enable the technician to quickly find lines of code that need to change. Technicians also use these tools to compare code with data files.

Further detailed investigation can be accomplished by using code restructuring and editing tools to cross reference lines of code and the use of data in multiple programs. And, of course, technicians can make the actual change in the logic of the program or in the database by using these tools.

In some situations, technicians are unable to make changes directly into the existing code or database. Instead, the only option is to rebuild a piece of the system. This is another gigantic problem that is easily overcome through the use of code generation tools.

Code generation tools are used to create databases from data structure diagrams and reports from report generation tools. There are tools in this category that make rebuilding user interfaces a snap.

And finally there are the testing tools. *Testing tools* make the tedious task of testing every aspect of your modified system a relatively painless ordeal. These are definitely tools that you need to have handy when you start testing all your systems at the same time.

Testing tools help generate and organize test data and make sure all the possible variations of data that can be passed through your system are used during the testing phase of the project.

And the most important feature of testing tools is their capability to simulate a typical and atypical data flow into your system. You can also use a testing tool to automatically enter data replicating a normal day's activities.

And Those Hard to Fix Problems

There are programs that cannot easily be fixed by your staff. Those programs are etched onto chips that run equipment that keeps your business operating. Let us examine some of these so you can appreciate the depth of the year 2000 bug on your business.

Some business operations require your employees to perform complex math problems using a calculator rather than a computer. Bond traders may frequently use a calculator to determine the current price of a long-term bond. The calculator that they use contains built-in functions that accept parameters—such as dates—then perform the calculation using the parameters and display the result on the screen.

Do these functions *accept* a four-digit year or do they *require* a 2-year digit? If the latter is the case, how will the calculator handle the year 00? This is something that your year 2000 team can easily check—or easily over look.

And bond traders are not the only people whose calculators perform critical functions. Anyone who uses a function on a calculator that calculates dates could be open to this same problem.

What is the fix? Buy a new calculator, one that is year 2000 compliant. The year 2000 bug is etched into the circuit board of old calculators and cannot be repaired.

Look around your office to find other circuit board or chip-driven hardware that could be date sensitive. Your elevators probably runs on a schedule that is maintained by a computer chip. This is how the elevator positions cars on strategic floors at peak times to dramatically cut down the wait time for your staff.

Fortunately many elevators are time sensitive rather than date sensitive. That is, elevator cars are moved into strategic floors at lunch time regardless of the date. Once the clock strikes noon, the car moves into position. These elevators are not affected by the year 2000 problem.

However, some sophisticated elevators may adjust the positions of the cars based on time and the day of the week. These elevators are affected since the day of the week is determined by the year. If the elevator uses a two-digit year, then what century is the year 00? If the year is 1900, then the first day of the year was a Monday. If the year is 2000, then the first day of the year is a Saturday. Will your elevators be on a Monday schedule or a Saturday schedule?

Of course, this problem continues throughout the year since the elevator is four days late every week. Fixing this problem depends on how the elevator was manufactured. If the timing mechanism is etched onto a circuit board or a chip, then you must contact the manufacturer to determine if a replacement board is available. If not, then there is little you can do to fix the problem.

On the other hand, the elevator might be software driven. The software resides on a small computer that can be adjusted either by the manufacturer replacing the software or by your staff entering data at the keyboard in response to software prompts. One prompt could be to select the current day. This fixes the problem immediately.

Your year 2000 team must examine all the equipment your firm owns to determine if the equipment is in any way date sensitive. We have just explored calculators and elevators, but you must also consider the equipment used to control the manufacturing process in your plant.

Then there is your building security. Is there an automatic expiration date assigned to every employee's keycard? Your security computer that tracks the movement of employees throughout your building could lock out some or all of your employees when the twenty-first century arrives.

This problem can be fixed by requesting a year 2000 upgrade from the vendor who supplied you with the software—assuming the vendor has an upgrade available. If not, you may need to consider switching vendors or you may need to install a different security system.

Another security problem affects your business and that of the law enforcement community. This involves date stamping on security cameras and video cameras used to record interrogations and for surveillance.

Say that the camera shows Tuesday and the year 00. What year is this? Is the day correct? And if the day and year is incorrect due to the year 2000 bug, will you need to bring an expert to court to prove the correct day and year?

As you can imagine, the repercussions of this, especially for law enforcement authorities, is dramatic. There is no easy fix other than replacing the equipment since the date mechanism that drives the time and day of week is located on the circuit board and cannot be changed.

Expect that any machine controlled by a computer circuit that is date sensitive cannot be repaired by your technical staff. You must rely on your vendors to upgrade the circuit board or you must acquire new control equipment for the machine. You probably do not have to replace the machine itself, only the equipment that contains the computer circuits.

Help Is There to Assist You

Do not assume that you are alone in dealing with the year 2000 problem. Everyone in business and government is confronting the same problem right now. And no one can ignore the problem because the year 2000 bug is there in your systems, and time will not chase the bug away.

Many businesses rely on service bureaus to provide equipment, service, and advice that is not readily available in house. These are your team members that fill in when your regular team falls down. You can expect that your team will stumble when addressing the year 2000 problem for your firm.

Therefore, prepare to bring in your hired support staff to come to the rescue. Nearly all of your service providers are tooled up to supply ancillary support at the ring of the telephone.

IBM, for example, has built a huge support effort to help their customers deal with the year 2000 problem. (Of course, some of their customers feel IBM was one of the major culprits that caused the problem in the first place). IBM offers a guidebook to help you through this process.

In addition, IBM is ready to move in their staff to solve the problem for you. IBM is not the only service company to offer this help. Major consulting and accounting firms are also prepared to offer a variety of services to your firm, from coaching your year 2000 team through the process to addressing your problem with their staff.

Bringing in the top guns is expensive especially if you feel that most of the problem was caused by faulty software and hardware supplied by vendors. Why should your firm pay for someone else's mistake? This issue is addressed in detail later in this book. However, this is a serious concern, one that can be influenced by pressure brought onto vendors. If your firm is important to a vendor's business, then you probably have strong leverage to persuade the vendor to fix the problem at the vendor's expense.

Unfortunately, not every firm is in such an influential position. But do not give up if you find yourself in such a position. Team up with other firms that use the vendor's services. They too have the same problem your firm faces. Collectively, you and your counterparts at the other firms can greatly influence the performance of the vendor to rectify the situation — without additional expenses to you, the vendor's customers.

A word of caution: The year 2000 problem is your firm's problem. Do not assume that you can buy a solution or force a vendor to solve the problem for your firm. If the vendor fails to deliver on its promise, then your problem does not go away. You still have to fix the problem—even if you decide to take legal action against the vendor.

The Bottom Line

Plan to launch a major, unprecedented effort to examine all your systems and all your equipment to determine how the year 2000 problem affects them. Determine the impact and prepare to spend a sizable amount of money that is not in your budget to fix this problem.

Everyone knows that your business is probably affected by the year 2000 bug. This includes your creditors, customers, your competition, and your stockholders, all of whom want to know what impact this condition could have on the performance of your business.

Furthermore, they want to know when this problem will hit your systems. Remember, systems that use future dates could try to calculate the year 00 today—and run into problems.

How do you plan to fix the year 2000 bug and what is the impact on your business if your plans do not succeed? These are two additional questions that your firm will be asked to answer. In the case of your creditors, your customers, and your stockholders, you had better be prepared to answer these questions proactively and without hesitation.

You can also use your plan as an edge over the competition by explaining how soon your systems will be year 2000 compliant—something your competitor may not be able to claim. Keep in mind that your customers' business depends on the continued operation of your business. And that is dependent on how well your firm resolves the year 2000 problem with all your systems.

Be aware that your competitor will probably jump at the chance to steal away your customers if you cannot answer their year 2000 inquires promptly and confidently. Expect that even your most loyal customer will quickly abandon your firm if there is any inkling that your systems lack of year 2000 compliance will threaten their business.

The clock is ticking and you have about 1000 days and even fewer business days to:

- Inventory all your systems and equipment;
- Assess the impact of the year 2000 bug on your firm;
- Develop a plan for rectifying the problem;
- Fix the problem;
- Test the new systems; and
- Implement the new systems.

Not much time is left and the deadline cannot be pushed back.

Don't Give Up Hope—Yet

I paint a bleak picture for the start of the twenty-first century. But it doesn't have to be this way if steps are taken immediately to lessen the impact, if any, the year 2000 bug has on your organization. There is still time to save your mission critical systems.

The question that begs answering is where to begin to attack this problem. First, there is no textbook approach that can be taken to assure your systems will be fixed by the turn of the century. This is a new problem of enormous proportions.

However, there are things that you can do to inventory your systems; tests you can perform to determine the likelihood that your systems will be affected by the year 2000 bug; and steps that you can take to remedy the problem.

The remaining chapters of this book address each step in the process and guide you through the massive task of protecting your computer systems and your business from the effect of the mother of all computer bugs.

And the Plot Thickens

Your investment in technology is about to go kaput in just a few short years and your technical staff may not even know the seriousness of the problem. As we move closer to welcoming the twenty-first century, your staff may be frozen in their tracks like a skunk in the road facing down the headlights of a Mack truck.

You better hope that your staff does not follow their instincts like the skunk who turns his back, raises his tail, and sprays—for the last time. For this is the best way for your company to become roadkill, something even the skunk realized too late.

The impact of the year 2000 problem is not appreciated by computer experts and business leaders. The problem is easy to understand, and this is probably what leads most to be naive and assume that the solution is just as easy to implement.

How difficult could the problem be if even the nontechnical kid can figure out the answer? Insert two digits everywhere the year is represented by two digits. You do not have to be an MIT graduate to derive this solution.

Avoid falling into this trap. By now you know that implementing this solution is something that takes a team of knowledgeable managers, technicians, and legal advisors months to investigate and years to resolve.

You can easily compare the magnitude of the year 2000 problem to landing on the moon. Anyone can look up in the sky and see the moon. Just take off in a rocket and steer the ship skyward and you are bound to land on the moon. If it were only that simple.

The year 2000 bug is a trap that coaxes you into a comfortable feel and lets you relax with a false sense of security. You do not realize that your company is in trouble until time has run out to address the problem. Right now you are in the headlights of the Mack truck, frozen in your tracks. And here are things that can happen when your firm becomes roadkill.

Renewal And Collection Notices Go Unsent

Consider for a moment a program that requires a date calculation to determine when to send you a notice that your drivers license is about to expire. The last time you renewed you drivers license was in 1999. The computer automatically determines when a year has transpired and therefore knows when a reminder notice must be generated.

Here are the business rules the programmer used to instruct the computer on how to arrive at this decision:

- Read the year of the date inside the computer (00).
- Subtract 1 from the year (00 minus 1).
- Find all the drivers whose driver's licenses were issued in that year (minus 1).

Wait! There is no year minus 1, so how can any renewal notices be generated? Without intervention, two likely scenarios could occur: The program could stop running altogether because the program came across an invalid year; or the program could carry out the instructions and search the electronic records and find that no driver's licenses require renewal.

Try telling this to the cop who stops you in the year 2000 and discovers that you are driving with an expired driver's license.

This is just the tip of the iceberg—a very big iceberg that can send large ripples through our cashless economy. The injury created by a lapse in notifying you that your driver's license should be renewed is minor. The worst that can happen is that you pay a fine, then renew your driver's license.

However, the more dramatic effect of an erroneous date calculation occurs with businesses whose computers fail to send notices of overdue invoices to their customers because the year 00 is not greater than the year 99—and there are no payments overdue, according to the computer.

Worse yet, problems with date fields in embedded hardware systems could cause such systems to malfunction. Missile guidance, radar, remote control, and other systems could all be affected.

Every business depends on a steady flow of money—rather a steady adjustment to the firm's electronic balance sheets. This occurs only if transactions are completed. For example, a firm provides a service or supplies goods to another firm and both companies adjust their books and records to reflect the transaction. In the old days, this meant a firm pays in cash.

What happens if the transaction flow is interrupted? If this occurs in many businesses, whole industries or the world economy could come to a grinding halt. This sounds fatalistic; however, following the logic of a transaction might give pause.

When a business manager needs to know which customer is delinquent, he or she asks for a report from the firm's database. The computer generates a report of all those accounts where the balance has not changed in over 30 days, 60 days, 90 days, and beyond, and where there is a payment due.

Say that today is March 5, 2000, and there is at least one account that has not paid since March 5, 1999. Many computer systems store these days as 030500 and 030599, dropping the century digits.

The task posed to the computer is this: Show me any account where today's date is greater than 90 days beyond the purchase date. The computer performs the subtraction, which results in the day and month digits being zero and the year digits being a minus 99. Since minus 99 is not greater than 90 days, no account is printed on the Accounts Overdue Report.

This means the business manager has no warning that a serious financial problem has occurred. After all, the computer never lies. If there are no overdue accounts, then the business is functioning well. Of course, we know better.

Imagine this occurring many times over in a single industry. The financial strength of the industry is in peril.

Wayward Reports

Business managers make important financial decisions based solely on the information provided to them in computer-generated reports. However, as illustrated in the previous section, rolling over the date to the year 2000 can cause unexpected and potentially lethal consequences to a business.

The logic used to select and display information on a report assumes the natural order of numbers where 0 is less than 9. Furthermore, this logic assumes that the year will never be greater than 1999—a wayward assumption.

Business managers and programmers apply this logic to the selection criteria of information for reports. For example, a report that lists sales in order of years works fine in 1999 but places sales figures for the year 2000 at the other end of the report, apparently out of sequence.

Some reports display the year 00 instead of 2000, and, therefore, 00 is the logical first number in the series, not the number that succeeds 99. And there's not much anyone can do to fix this problem quickly. The only sure fix is to use all the digits in the year and, as you will see later in this book, the task of inserting these two digits is complicated and time consuming.

A more puzzling problem arises when a report displays the full year (2000), however, the date and the associated information is placed out of sequence just as if the year was stored as 00. How can this be since the full year is used in the report?

The problem stems from the fact that the sort order of the report is determined by a special file called an index file. An index file is like an index to a book where keywords are placed in alphabetical order along with reference to pages that contain all the information related to the keyword. The computer references the location of the related information in the database file rather than by page.

The computer that generates a report might only use two digits to represent the year in the index file, which causes perfectly logical information for the year 2000 to be displayed out of sequence in a report.

Error Detection Gone Crazy

Programmers often write code that tells the computer how to identify suspicious data. One of these tests is to determine if the year is substantially less than 99 such as 00. If so, the computer is told to reject the data and perhaps stop running the program.

Glancing at this idea raises questions about the rationale for such assumptions. How could anyone, especially a computer programmer, reach such a conclusion? Looking back, we can see the flaw in this logic but in the late 1960s and on through the 1980s and even the early 1990s, programmers saw this problem a different way.

The year 2000 was so far away that the digits that represent the year 00 were more likely to be data errors than real years. Surely by the time 2000 rolled around, this program would be obsolete. So it was safe to consider such data to be in error. And they couldn't be bothered with the programming that would be required to get around this problem. So the digits were used as a sign of trouble and programmers told the computer to take evasive action when erroneous data was encountered.

Of course, come the year 2000, data that was once suspicious will no longer be invalid data. However, the logic to trap suspicious data still exists somewhere in the millions of lines of instruction that run every day on computers throughout the world.

Forecasting Gone Sour

Forecasting is the art of finding mathematical relationships among historical data that can be used to predict the future. We have seen attempts to forecast the weather, automobile sales, and even which horse is going to win the next race. Some predictions are relatively successful while others miss their mark.

However, businesses, governments, and the scientific community use these statistical models to make serious decisions that affect millions of lives and risk billions of dollars on the outcome.

Historical data used to develop these forecasting models are series of raw data stored by year in a computer database. Until recently when programmers realized the hazards of representing a year with two digits, data series were identified by a two-digit year.

You already appreciate the problems that this causes in other computer applications that we have talked about in this chapter. In this case, there can be confusion as to whether data identified as year 00 is empirical data of 1900 or 2000.

The difference can be significant and can have a dramatic effect on the forecasting ability of the computer application. The mathematical relationship between data recorded in 1900 and data recorded in 2000 is drastically different.

Computer Shutdowns

When most of us think about computer programs we conjure the image of application programs. These are programs that are designed to make the computer do something useful for us. Those that come to mind are Microsoft Word and Excel and the payroll program that makes sure that we get paid on a regular schedule.

There are other kinds of programs that are not application programs. These are programs such as those found in the operating system. An operating system is a group of programs that makes the box of switches that we call a computer able to run application programs.

For example, a program in the operating system time stamps the date and time on your files. Another program calculates the time and date for the internal clock and calendar for your computer which are used by many application programs to determine the current date and time.

Still another kind of program used in the operation of large computers is an archival program, which automatically makes a copy of program files and data files and stores them on tape. These files can be restored from tape if the files used by the computer become corrupt and disabled.

The question that computer professionals must ask is how will critical, nonapplication programs handle the date rollover to the twenty-first century? This question must be answered since improper handling of the date can affect every program running on the computer.

Some operating system programs might recognize the year 00 as a fatal error, one that halts the operation of the computer. And the program that recognizes this date as an error might be encoded onto a computer chip that is not easy for staff programmers to correct.

This raises another question: Will application programs recognize the year 00 on a time stamp of a file as a valid date or the current year in the computer's internal clock as a valid date?

Furthermore, some archival programs might recognize the date 00 or 99 as a signal not to archive the current files, which could be disastrous.

Incorrect Calculations

Accuracy of the information is a more serious problem than information being in the wrong place on the report. There are two reasons why people and businesses place money in a bank: for security, knowing someone else must make good on the money if the money is missing; and to earn interest on the money.

The bank is able to pay interest because your money is loaned to others who pay the bank interest for the use of money. The difference between what the bank charges for interest and what the bank pays in interest to account holders is part of the profit bankers earn.

The amount of money that is earned or paid for the use of money (interest) is determined by a calculation. Simply, an annual rate of interest is applied to the length of time the money is borrowed by either the bank from account holders or from customers from the bank.

By now you probably suspect the problem. The problem lies with the calculation that is used to determine the length of time that the money is borrowed. This calculation is probably performed by a computer program. The question that needs to be answered is, does this program use all four digits of the date or just the two that represent the year?

The answer to this question has a dramatic impact on the results of the calculation. Say that the loan was for the time period between 1999 and 2000. The program subtracts 1999 from 2000 for a loan period of 1 year.

What if the program only used the last two digits of the year in the calculation? The program subtracts 99 from 00 for a loan period of minus 99 years. Will the program stop running because of this strange result? Will the program keep running—and not pay the interest due?

The impact of this error can be life threatening to the financial industry. Imagine if no account holder receives interest for a substantial period of time. They would contact the bank for an explanation. However, the banking industry does not have enough staff to address the inquiries. In recent years, bankers reduced staff and relied on computers to address inquiries from customers.

Will customers then withdraw their funds from the bank? This is the next logical step. This is called a run on the bank—when customers come in mass to make withdrawals—something that was last seen in this country during the savings and loan crisis, a period when many savings and loan banks were forced out of business.

And how can bankers make a quick recovery? At the turn of the last century, bankers manually adjusted interest payments in ledger books. Now the ledger book is replaced by computer-generated reports. The staff that is necessary to make manual interest adjustments to all the accounts no longer exists. Simply, there is no quick fix after the mother of all bugs strikes.

Some readers may feel this is fatalistic and the impact exaggerated. I hope they are correct and I am wrong. This scenario I played out is simply following the logical reaction of account holders when interest they are promised is not paid on schedule.

We are talking about an incorrect calculation in interest. How many other date-sensitive calculations are used in mission critical programs for industry and government?

Many businesses order supplies based on comparisons of the previous year's empirical data against the current year's business. For example, a typical question asked every day in business is, how much inventory did we have on hand on October 5, 1999, and what were sales at that time?

If the sales level for this year (2000) is approximately the same sales level as last year (1999), then there is a high probability, barring a disaster, that inventory for October 5, 2000, should be approximately the same as the inventory for October 5, 1999.

An owner of a mom-and-pop business would look at the books from last year to make this comparison and arrive at an expected inventory level for this year. However, managers of large businesses rely on computers to make this decision for them.

A programmer writes instructions to have the computer compare sales figures for the same period of time and then, if they are similar, the computer is told to order inventory to meet the inventory level for the same period as the previous year.

Whether or not the program successfully completes this mission depends on whether the program uses two or four digits to represent the year in the calculation.

The program determines last year by subtracting one from the current year. If the current year is 2000, then the previous year is 1999. However if the current year is 00, then the previous year is minus 1. There is no inventory for the year minus 1 because minus 1 is not a valid year. Will the computer know this?

....

The Wrong Day of the Week

How important is it to your business that your computer programs know the current day of the week? If this is critical to the survival of your business, then you better begin to work fast to correct this next problem.

The new century begins on Saturday, January 1, 2000; that is, unless the computer programs use only two digits to represent the year. Then, the new century begins on Monday, January 1, 2000.

Are you a little confused? You shouldn't be, because this makes perfect sense. Many computer programs make the assumption that the year 00 means 1900. Until just recently, this was a fair assumption to make—by short-sighted programmers who thought their programs would not be running into the next century.

The first day of the century in 1900 was a Monday. Therefore, many computer programs assume that the dates and days of the twentieth century are the same as the dates and days of the twenty-first century.

The impact of this problem can be very interesting—and costly to business. First, the day the payroll checks are written by the computer is off by one day or six days, depending on how the program is written.

When will the computer write the check to pay the company's bills? Computers age invoices. This means that a computer program determines the most economical time to pay the bill. For example, some firms give customers a discount if the invoice is paid within ten days. Some firms begin to charge customers interest if the invoice is not paid within 30 days.

In large firms, computer programs determine the most advantageous time to write the check. For example, checks might be written on a Friday knowing that a customer will not be able to deposit the check until the following Monday. But what day is Friday? It depends on whether the current year is 1900 or 2000.

Cash Flow in Peril

Nearly every business relies heavily on a dependable cash flow, especially those business that are undercapitalized. Cash on hand—really a number that represents a dollar amount in the bank's computer—is the safety net for many firms even in a good economy.

Businesses are prepared to float an amount that a customer owes for up to 60 days without becoming overly concerned about receiving payment. However, if nearly all of a firm's customers stretch payments out to the maximum limit, then a serious drain on the firm's cash reserves can result.

The system begins to break down. No steady income and no cash reserves means the firm's bills will not be paid and soon there is no business and no business partners.

What does this have to do with the year 2000 bug? Everything! Practically all payments made to businesses today are in the form of electronic transfer. That is, one computer sends another computer a file that is used to adjust each firm's book entry system.

As illustrated in the previous section, payments are generated by a firm's computerized accounting system according to business rules that are called *aging payables*. The foundation of this theory is for a firm to hold onto the firm's money until the last minute, when the bills must be paid.

Keep in mind that the firm's money is housed in an interest-bearing account in a financial institution and gathering interest daily. Basically, the firm is making money on the firm's money, so the business manager is not willing to lose this earning power until the last minute.

Fortunately, all businesses consider the aging of payables in their pricing structure and as long as the flow of cash is predictable, businesses and their business partners survive. However, the flow of payments to businesses might be disrupted by the mother of all bugs. What day of the week is the payment due? And what year was that? You have seen how computer programs are expected to be fooled into arriving at the wrong date information. If this occurs to the aging programs in many businesses, then the flow of funds can come to a screeching halt.

The repercussion of such a monumental incident creates a serious ripple effect in undercapitalized businesses. When the funds dry up from customers, business managers find themselves between a rock and a hard place.

Most customers expect to continue to receive service from the firm while they sort out the computer glitch. And the business manager wants to cooperate for fear of losing a good customer.

On the other hand, without receiving payments from customers, there are very few businesses who can continue to give away their services and stay in business. So what will happen?

The firm's cash reserves are used first, then the business manager turns to banks and factoring firms to convert receivables into money. This costs the firm money and could actually make a once profitable customer into a money loser.

Multiply this scenario over and over again with each customer and soon the business is in bankruptcy. When one undercapitalized firm goes under, the rest are sure to follow.

Am I overstating the negative of a bad situation? I hope I am. But the reality is that unless aging programs are fixed by the start of the twenty-first century, the flow of payments among firms will be disrupted. And most firms will delay payments to vendors until the computer glitch is repaired.

The Case of…the Consultants

Building computer programs for your business is a costly affair. Programs are a necessary piece of every business. In theory, the more automated a business becomes, the more cost efficient a business can grow and realize great financial rewards.

When a business manager is faced with the need for a new computer system, one of these options is chosen: hire a programmer, buy software off the shelf, or hire temporary employees called consultants to write the system.

One case involved a growing service company in the northeast that specialized in promotional packaging for consumer manufacturers. They were always able to come up with ways to package any promotional idea that an advertising agency could dream up.

A key reason for the rapid growth and profitability of the firm was the owner's ability to minimize full-time staff. She placed all her financial resources in her sales staff and her idea people, which she called her "brain trust." These were the men and woman who tackled the problems brought in by the sales staff.

When it came time for the firm to computerize the business, they turned to a handful of outside consultants. The owner hired them through a consulting firm who specialized in finding jobs of short duration for computer professionals. Consultants are instant experts in a particular language or type of computer. They know how to come into a firm, size up a project quickly, and build a computer system.

Once the system is built, the consultants leave and are usually never seen again. This seemed the most economical approach for this promotional packaging company. In and out quickly. It was their way of doing business.

However, within a few years their systems became unmanageable. They were held together by a thread of luck. Each consultant came in and slapped some code together almost anywhere they could fit it into the system. The consultant got the system to do what the owner expected, then left a mess for someone else to clean up.

But the owner of the business did not realize the sloppiness of her computer systems. They were in a sad state of affairs. And then she read about the year 2000 problem. Once again she called in a consultant who just shook his head and described to her in layman's terms that she would be better off if she rebuilt the system from scratch. He said that over the years various consultants patched the system rather than integrating changes the proper way into the system. This resulted in spaghetti code—a lot of ends, each beginning a process that ends somewhere unexpectedly.

....

Costly Fix

How much are you willing to spend to fix the year 2000 problem? And if you are not willing to spend this amount, how do you plan to survive? Implementing the solution to the year 2000 problem is an expensive proposition that can run into the millions of dollars for a small corporation. You probably cannot continue in business much past the year 2000 if you are unwilling—or cannot afford—to pay the repair bill.

A recent report in the press indicated that a company spent 12 weeks conducting a survey of all the corporate systems to understand the scope of this problem. The results were alarming. There were 100 systems (individual groups of programs that controlled an aspect of the business) that were used to run the business. About 20 of these systems would stop working in the year 2000 because of dates represented as two digits.

These 20 systems were critical systems to the company. In total, these 20 systems represented 9000 individual programs and about 3500 databases. Think of the massive problem that lies ahead for this firm. Theoretically, the computer department would have to stop all projects, triple the staff, and focus all their attention on fixing the problem.

This fix has a steep price tag that must be paid. It is very difficult to quantify the cost of such an undertaking. Industry does not have any experience with such a vast change in computer systems. However, some in the press estimate the cost could be higher than $100 million for a typical, large corporation.

Just consider what is involved in finding what needs to be fixed, then fixing and testing it. You need programmers, lots of programmers, since all the changes must be in production before New Year's Eve, 1999. And since programmers are usually smart people, they realize that there is no long-term future with the firm, so they will demand—and receive—top wages for their work.

Those programmers need some place to work. This requires firms to rent and furnish offices. If a firm doubles or triples the firm's programmers, the firm can expect a substantial increase in the need for computer resources.

Programmers also need software tools to help them fix this problem. Those tools are probably not in your software inventory so they must be purchased and installed, and your programmers must be trained in the use of these tools.

Since this problem is not isolated to a business or industry, businesses can expect a run on computer resources. Every business needs these resources today—expect delays.

Of course, all this additional expense is reflected on the bottom line. And the saddest fact is that no business or government can avoid paying for this problem.

Who Is Going to Pay?

As I pointed out, the problem stems from a combination of poor economics, sloppy programming, and the failure of some programming tools. These are fighting words to those in the legal profession, especially when businesses are faced with paying a substantial amount to prevent a catastrophic loss.

Many of the programs were built by the firms themselves so there is no one to blame except managers who probably left the firm long ago. Some companies purchased software from vendors and others contracted with vendors to build proprietary software for the firm.

In these cases, some may say that the vendor is liable for the failure of the software, therefore, the vendor should pay to fix the problem. As you will read in Chapter 3, which discusses the legal aspect of this problem, vendors counter this argument by saying that the problem was known by the firms when they acquired the software.

Another avenue of attack can be against vendors who supplied programming tools such as compilers that limited the representation of a year to two digits. In some cases, these compilers were the only tools that translated source code to executable code for that brand of computer. Programmers had no choice but to accept the limitation and use the compiler to build programs that were bound to fail in the year 2000.

Some blame compiler and computer manufacturers such as IBM, Computer Associates, and DEC for starting the problem. Although the reasoning behind programmers excluding the century digit in dates to save resources seems sound, the question remains as to why there was a limitation imposed on the tools used by those programmers. These tools stifled programmers' capabilities to use the century date.

Furthermore, there is the question of whether or not the tool and computer manufacturers made this limitation known—and its negative impact—when the tools were sold. This raises a number of legal issues regarding responsibility for paying for the repair and paying for any collateral damage that is realized because of the shortcomings of these tools.

Although this point is addressed in the chapter that explores the legal ramifications of this problem, firms should not expect a legal remedy to protect their business from being adversely affected by the mother of all bugs.

The bug is in your programs, those programs that you depend on to run your business. And the bug will cause havoc beginning January 1, 2000, regardless of who is responsible for the problem.

The Case of ... This Is My Vendor's Problem

A local government agency in the northwest hired an outside firm to provide computerized accounting services. The contract with the company called for the agency to send all the paperwork for purchases, payroll, and other financial matters to the company's offices where the data was entered into the company's computers.

The company kept the electronic books and records of the agency and wrote checks to pay the agency's vendors. It didn't take long before the company talked the agency staff into entering the data themselves into the company's computers via a terminal in the agency's office connected to the company's computer by telephone lines.

....

Losing Your Financing

The cost factor in solving the year 2000 problem is a killer. This is money that is not in your business plans, not in your current budget or projected budgets five years hence. This additional expense can have a major impact on your business operations, second only to the effects of the year 2000 bug itself.

Like most businesses you probably project earnings based on expected sales and expenses. Earnings projection are used to determine asset acquisitions, staffing, and other key ingredients that are needed to maintain current sales levels and growth.

These projects are used to determine your financing requirements. Cash flow supplies the capital necessary to meet only a portion of the immediate financial needs for most firms. Creditors must be encouraged to supply the rest of the financing in the form of short-, medium-, and long- term loans.

However, creditor financing is only available if they believe in the sales, expense, and earnings projections. With the year 2000 problem lurking over your company, expect creditors to examine your business plans closely to determine if rectifying this problem is included in your plans.

If not, then chances are your creditors will not continue to provide the financing required to keep you business afloat—and supply the money that is necessary to make your systems year 2000 compliant.

Furthermore, your present financing agreements could be in jeopardy. Business plans presented to creditors two, three, and four years ago that were used to secure current financing probably did not include anything about the year 2000 problem.

This could be viewed as fraudulently acquiring financing for your firm, although this is stretching the circumstances a lot. At a minimum, the absence of addressing this problem could have a major impact on your business plans and could cause creditors to invoke an escape clause. Typical such clauses are written into financing agreements which allow the creditor to back out of the deal if major factors influencing the business were not made known at the time the agreement was signed. Do not mislead yourself in thinking ignorance of the problem will protect you with your creditors. When times get tough and friendships are put aside, your creditors could state that the industry knew of the problem when the credit agreement was signed. This is hard to deny. Therefore, since the industry "knew" about the problem, you should have known too. Based on this reasoning, you are at fault. Your ignorance will save you from any civil or criminal action, but this will surely place you on shaky ground when trying to enforce the existing credit agreement.

Your only recourse is to consult with your attorney, then decide how your firm is going to address this problem and present this information to your creditors—now. Your forthrightness will help to continue to strengthen your working relationship with creditors, a relationship that you have built up over the years. You are going to need their assistance to finance the repair of your systems.

Containing The Cost

You must present a realistic financing plan for your business and for the year 2000 project. The cost of the year 2000 fix is substantial; however, you can take special precautions to contain the cost. These techniques are fully explained in later chapters, but we will touch on some of them here.

Leverage support that vendors are willing to provide free of charge or at a minimum expense. Some vendors realize that software sold to you is not year 2000 compliant. Whether or not they are willing to admit full responsibility for fixing the problem is a question their lawyers will probably answer.

But that does not mean that you will not be able to make arrangements to have them help you resolve this issue. You could volunteer your site for use by the vendor to find and fix the problem with the software. The out-of-pocket cost to you is negligible, yet you acquire the full attention of the vendor. In exchange for your assistance, the vendor might waive any upgrade cost that is passed along to customers.

You can contain the cost of refurbishing your home-built software by carefully assessing the changes that must be made to the system and databases. Simply said, you do not have to change all the dates used in your system to be year 2000 compliant.

Dates used for database indexes, data sorting, and date calculations are the only dates that need to be modified. The rest of the dates can probably remain as they are and will not affect your business operations. This technique can dramatically reduce the time that is needed to repair your systems.

Small routines called bridge programs (more on this later in the book) can quickly be built to handle date transformation on the fly. Bridge programs are used to change the format of dates coming from a non complaint system and going to a compliant system, assuming the dates that your system is sending are not compliant. In both cases, dates in your systems remain unchanged.

Another method of cost containment is to scale your technical staff based on the tasks that need to be accomplished. Simply said, an entry-level programmer can make most of the code changes while a more experienced programmer is needed to locate the lines of code that need fixing. Compensation for an entry-level programmer is much lower than that of an experienced programmer. This difference shows up in the bottom line cost of the year 2000 project.

These are just a few of the ways you can reduce the expense of fixing your systems. Other techniques are covered in detail later in this book.

Above all, avoid overreacting to the scope of the problem and, therefore, writing a blank check to fix the problem. Everyone who is willing to help you, such as vendors, consulting firms, and technicians, are under the impression that your firm is between a rock and a hard place and that you are willing to pay anything to get things back to normal.

However, this is not necessarily the case. Careful project and expense planning can move your firm into a strong negotiating position and reduce the overall cost for bringing your systems into year 2000 compliance.

Inside the Government

Now if you think your business is facing a nightmarish calamity in the making, wait until you hear what is in store for the federal government. Computer programs are used by government officials to perform assorted functions including many that are critical to the stability of our economy and our national security.

Let's take government entitlement programs that provide a net to catch us when we are down on our luck. These are the same entitlement programs that are the largest portion of the federal budget and the segment that is growing, some say, beyond the taxpayers' capabilities to pay for the programs.

Many of the entitlement programs determine a person's eligibility by calculating the person's age. Isn't this the same calculation that I used earlier in this chapter to illustrate the year 2000 problem? If the government's computer cannot accurately calculate a person's age, then how will the government know if a person is entitled to the benefits of a program?

The fallout of just this single miscalculation can be devastating. Some persons who qualify might be rejected by the computer. Others might take advantage of this problem and connive their way into receiving benefits that they shouldn't receive. This could lead to inflation of the entitlement rolls and an artificial increase in the cost of running these programs, and there might be no practical way to rectify the problem.

The government computers are also used to transfer funds electronically to and from government accounts at financial institutions. The timing and amounts of these transfers are dependent on dates in a computer. If the date is wrong and the transfer is mistaken, will it be possible to have an accurate accounting of government funds? Keep in mind that the federal government is probably the largest consumer in our economy and failure to make timely payment of government debt can have a negative ripple effect throughout our economy and the world economy.

This is an exaggeration—or is it? Many foreign investors make substantial purchases of government bonds. That is, foreign investors loan money to the federal government so government officials can pay bills.

Of course, for this generosity the federal government returns the money with interest.

Interest is paid according to a schedule, a schedule that is maintained by a program running on a government computer. The same computer that could have sitting inside of it the mother of all bugs just waiting for the stroke of midnight, January 1, 2000.

What would happen if the federal government missed an interest payment? Unless treasury officials moved quickly, foreign and domestic investors would probably sell their government bonds in the market place. Prices of these securities would plummet.

And the next time the federal government needs to borrow funds—once a month—the interest demanded by the marketplace would be unthinkable. Why would the government expect to pay such high interest rates? Because the government defaulted on paying their current outstanding debt. Why could this have happened? Because the computer program that issues the interest checks miscalculated the due date. I hope that this scenario is farfetched. However, technically this scenario outcome is possible.

I will stop with the entitlement programs and the treasury issues. It would be easy for me to continue with other areas of the federal government including the defense department, the FBI, the CIA, and even NASA.

Fortunately, the issue is well known to the U.S. government. However, many foreign governments are not reacting to the problem. In addition, international corporations have been very slow to react to this problem. The problem will most likely be worse outside of the United States.

The Case of...The Boss Doesn't Know

The head of a large petroleum company on the West Coast started to give stern warnings after he uncovered a deception with the administrative executives of his firm. Like many large corporations, the chain of command mirrored that of the military and the politics within the command structure rivaled any presidential race. The first rule of corporation politics is not to be the bearer of bad news. Those in authority always confuse the messenger as being responsible for the message, which usually means immediate dismissal.

When the head of the firm began reading about the year 2000 problem in the media, he asked the executive responsible for administration for an impact report."How will this bug affect the operation of the company?"

An almost immediate response came back. "We have it all under control. There will be no negative impact to our operations."

Of course, the initial question caused executives down the chain of command to quietly and quickly learn about the problem. "What year 2000 bug?" they could be heard whispering the executive wash room.

Although the president of the firm received the answer he was looking for, no one actually investigated the potential problem within the computer department of the firm. The question filtered down the chain of command and each executive responded positively as if everything was under control—and then wondered what each was talking about.

The Crooks May Get a Break

Most of the discussion about the year 2000 problem centers around business and governmental operations and how this bug can cause havoc in a matter of a second. Also affected by this problem are the law enforcement and judicial systems.

You have already seen how the automatic date and time stamp on a police surveillance camera can report the wrong year and the wrong day of the week once the new century rolls around. A defense attorney is likely to question the police officer on the stand:

"Officer, your reports accuses my client of committing the crime on Saturday, January 1, 2000. Is that correct?"

"Yes."

"But the video camera that recorded the crime, committed by someone who resembles my client, reported that the crime occurred on a Monday. Who is wrong?"

You can envision how Perry Mason would have a good time using this bug to create a hole in the prosecution's case. And who knows how juries will react to conflicting evidence.

Enough about the year 2000 problem affecting evidence in a case. Let us turn our attention to the computer systems that are used to track those convicted of a crime. Say a criminal is sentenced to five years in prison in 1997 (and assume this is federal prison where nearly all of the sentence is served). All the information including the release date is probably entered in some computer.

Each month the computer prints a list of those prisoners who are eligible for release. So in the year 02, our prisoner's name appears on this list—or does it? The year 02 is not five years beyond 1997. It is probably 95 years before 1997. If you are confused, so will the computer be.

We have not yet addressed how computers are used in the parole system nor how they are used by judges when they check on the criminal records of accused and convicted persons. Will the year 2000 problem cause such confusion over criminal records that judges and others in law enforcement will make mistakes? Will these mistakes cause undue harm to the innocent and undue benefit to the guilty?

Unless those who are responsible for those systems act quickly to determine the impact of the bug, all of us will find out the answers to these questions starting with the first day of the new century.

The Lack of Awareness

What adds fuel to the concerns that the worst case scenarios I mention in this chapter might come to fruition is that very few people are doing anything about solving this problem. In fact, few government and business leaders realize the seriousness of the year 2000 bug. This was pointed out in a recent survey made by Congress. Only six agencies of the federal government had estimated the cost of fixing this bug in their computer programs. The other agencies are just beginning to plan how they are going to approach this problem.

Published reports state that the Social Security Administration and the Department of Defense are not close to having a finished inventory of their programs to determine the scope of the problem. NASA does not expect to have a plan for fixing the problem in place before the end of the first quarter of 1997.

What is frightening about this is that some government officials feel that every computer program must be inventoried and fixed by 1998. This provides time for testing the changes before the twenty-first century begins.

Some departments of federal government, such as the Department of Transportation, did not respond to the congressional survey. This includes the Federal Aviation Administration, which is responsible for air safety. Then other departments such as the Department of Energy are just starting to research the problem—shortly after receiving the survey form from Congress.

And if that was not bad enough, some systems running today are already using the year 2000 and beyond in date calculations. This means that the results of those calculations are questionable—but no one is questioning them. Hopefully, technicians patched these systems to accept date into the new century but no one knows for sure.

Although there are no firm cost figures, some officials are estimating that fixing this one bug will cost the federal government $30 billion. And all this work fixing the problem must go on while government officials continue daily operations.

Let's not be too harsh on the federal government for dropping the ball. Published reports have estimated that in the United States alone about 30% of businesses recognize this potential problem and have begun taking action to stamp out the bug. This means at least 70% of businesses still do not recognize that a potentially serious and fatal disaster lurks just on the other side of the twentieth century.

Ignorance, corporate politics, or the business leaders' comfort with personal computer software could be the reason for this apparent lack of concern. The solution to the problem is easily understood by the layperson. Two digits are missing and this oversight will screw up important calculations. When this occurs on a spreadsheet, you just drag the column over and insert the two missing digits. If it were only that easy.

Business and government leaders do not appreciate the dilemma facing them. Their computer departments are facing one of the most complex undertakings they have ever attempted. This project is unlike typical programming projects in that the deadline is immovable and a missed deadline can produce unthinkable results.

Consider these statistics. Only about 15% of all programming projects are completed on time and this is under normal conditions working with a familiar set of factors. The year 2000 bug presents unfamiliar factors that will challenge even the sharpest computer department.

The Old Software Ain't Like It Used to Be

Your old reliable software that you purchased off the shelf years ago may be headed for the scrap heap along with older computers. The problem is that many companies have not upgraded their personal computers nor personal computer software such as word processing and spreadsheet packages.

The question that needs to be answered is how will these software packages—and older computers—be affected by the year 2000 problem. I am talking about the 286 computers and older word processing software like WordStar.

At one time these were the most popular combinations in business and in home computing. Millions feel that if these products continue to work fine that there is no need to throw them away and buy new, expensive software and hardware.

As strange as this sounds, this combination and similar ones are still in use in business. Daily operations depend on accurate data being produced by this software and hardware. Now a new century is coming and the old reliable software and hardware may not work properly with the new date.

Be prepared to replace your older equipment with newer personal computers such as the Pentium series, the PowerPC, Windows 95, and Windows NT. All of these are year 2000 compliant today. Many of the popular software products such as Word for Windows and Excel are also ready for the year 2000.

The Quick Acid Test

Ask a few pointed questions to the managers of your computer department to find out if your organization is in a good position to combat the year 2000 bug. Here they are:

1. How many systems are operational in the firm?

2. How many of those systems are mission critical?

3. How many individual programs make up those mission critical systems?

4. How many lines of instructions, on the average, are there in each of those programs?

5. Where is the source code for each program that makes up those mission critical systems?

6. How many of those mission critical systems are affected by the year 2000 bug?

7. Is there a plan for fixing the year 2000 bug?

8. Is there a contingency plan if the fix is not in place in time?

9. How much will it cost to fix the year 2000 bug?

10. Have the firm's business partners addressed this problem yet?

You might be shocked at the answers you receive. Consider that 1997 is here and January 1, 2000, is less than three years away. Can your computer department complete the largest programming project that they have ever attempted—tested and fully implemented—in three years?

Examining Those Hidden Computers

Start now with a cursory review of everything in your business that can be affected by the year 2000 problem. Begin with the acid test, then continue with a close look at those easily overlooked computers: those that run your elevators; those that perform calculations; and those that protect your building.

How are your elevators affected by the date change? This is a rather easy question to answer. Call the manufacturer of your elevators or the service company that maintains the elevators and ask them. Within a matter of minutes you will know if there is a potential problem and, if so, whether the problem can be fixed by entering a new date into the existing software; acquiring a software upgrade; or replacing a circuit board. You will also learn the degree of support the elevator manufacturer is providing existing customers to solve the year 2000 problem.

Assessing the impact of calculators is an easier task than calling the elevator manufacturer. Here's what you do:

- Identify all built-in functions in the calculator that require you to pass the function a date.
- Find functions that return dates.
- Test these functions by passing 00 as the year.
- Continue the test by passing 2000 as the year.
- A final test is to pass data that causes the function to return a date beyond the year 1999.

Any problems that you would experience after the turn of the century are sure to make an appearance right now. Within a few minutes you will know if you must toss out the calculator and buy a new one—one that is already year 2000 compliant.

Next, examine your security cameras and other building security devices. Do they show the century digits? If not, then they would probably be tainted as evidence in court and would require a smart attorney to rectify the legal problem. Simply review last night's videotape from the security camera to learn if the security system is affected by the year 2000 bug.

Then you will need to examine the software that runs your employee identification system. Find out if the system is date sensitive and, if so, how the system will handle the change of century. A call to the manufacturer of the system should answer this question.

Your survey should identify all kinds of equipment with built-in circuitry that could be influenced by date changes. If you are unsure whether or not a piece of equipment should be added to the list, then add it to the list. Unfortunately, finding out if these devices are affected by the year 2000 problem is not as straightforward. The best way is to give a call to the manufacturer and ask if the device is year 2000 compliant.

Likely Places to Look for Trouble

Where do you begin looking for places where the year 2000 bug can hide? Throughout the first two chapters we explored areas that are prone to the year 2000 bug. We will take a more formal approach in tracking down this problem throughout the rest of this book.

For now let us take a quick look at a more complete list of trouble spots for your company. The key for a system to make this list is that the system is sensitive to date and day of the week. A system that is only time sensitive should not be affected by the problem because time is not directly connected to the date stored inside your computer.

The list begins with systems that are found in a typical corporation. These include:

- Invoice systems;
- Payroll systems;
- Inventory systems;
- Databases where information is looked up by date or day of the week;
- Any system that sorts data based on the date;
- Credit card transaction systems;
- Bill payment systems;
- Personnel systems;

- Security systems;

- Source code management systems used in the computer depart-ment; and

- Telephone systems.

This is far from an exclusive list of systems since many corporations have industry related systems like:

- Trade entry systems in the securities industry;

- Loan portfolio systems in the banking industry;

- Point-of-purchase systems in the retail industry; and

- Medical record systems in the medical industry.

You can add to both lists without giving much thought to identifying systems in your firm that could be affected by this problem. Of course, the computers themselves and office software must also be placed on the list of suspects. These include:

- The operating system that runs your computers;

- The ROM BIOS chip inside your computer that enables you to boot your computer;

- Old—and not so old—office software the runs on your personal computer.

And you may not think twice about the problem affecting your old office software such as your spreadsheets, word processor, and desktop data-bases. The solution is as simple as buying new software.

This does get rid of the year 2000 problem. Instead, another problem is cre-ated. That old software created files that may not be usable by the new soft-ware. Your old spreadsheets could have macros that save you countless hours of work, but have to be rewritten into the new spreadsheet software. And the person who wrote the original macros is no longer employed with your firm.

Probably the biggest headache comes when you replace your desktop database software. It is not unusual to find that a mission critical appli-cation runs on a desktop database. Code written to run the application is normally written in a language that is unique to the old database software. For example, the Paradox Application Language (PAL) was used to created applications for the Paradox desktop database software.

The problem that occurs is that in many cases the code is not transportable to the new database software. This means that someone must rebuild the desktop application using the new database software language. You end up with a quick solution to the year 2000 problem, but face the time-consuming task of recreating complex macros and applications.

Here are a few other software packages to be concerned about:

cc:Mail, the popular mail software, runs on a number of different platforms. However, at this writing, only cc:Mail for Windows (the R6 version) is year 2000 compliant. Other versions of cc:Mail for Windows and cc:Mail running on other platforms are not compliant and must be upgraded.

Lotus Notes is year 2000 compliant. However, you must be careful about how you enter dates. You can always enter a four-digit year. If you are using a version of Lotus Notes prior to release 4.5, then Lotus Notes assumed that all two-digit years are in the twentieth century. With the beginning of release 4.5, two-digit years that are between 50 and 99 are assumed to be in the twentieth century and years between 00 and 49 are assumed to be in the twenty-first century. No assumption is made when you use the date function (@Date). Therefore, you should always use the four-digit year with this function.

Lotus 1-2-3 release 5 for Windows and release 4 for DOS are the first versions that are year 2000 compliant, according to published reports. Two-digit years are assumed to be in the twentieth century and four-digit years are taken literally.

IBM computers such as the S/390, AS/400, RISC/6000, and the PowerPC are year 2000 complaint. So are all IBM personal computers and personal computer servers that were introduced after January 1, 1996. However, older models may not be in compliance. Some machines may require you to run a utility program to fix the problem or update the century manually at the keyboard.

And Now for Some Long, Hard Work

There are less than a thousand days left before the turn of the clock inside your computer welcomes in either a great century or the worst time in your life. The deadline is approaching and you and your staff have some difficult work ahead of you.

Fortunately, you are not alone. Computer and software manufacturers such as IBM realize the deficiencies of older products and have taken the initiative to develop a wide range of tools that can help you. These tools are reviewed later in this book.

In addition to tools, manufacturers are working hard to build upgrades to replace the outdated equipment and software that you are currently running. Do not expect to receive this free of charge, but the price that you pay is worth paying because this solves a key problem that confronts your firm.

The remainder of this book takes you step by step through the process of making sure that your firm does not fall victim to the year 2000 problem. There are no shortcuts. The road ahead is a long, winding maze filled with traps and dead ends that wait for the opportunity to scuttle your efforts to save your company.

In the remaining chapters, we lay out the path that you can follow to reach the end of this road in the shortest time and achieve your goal— getting your business ready for the twenty-first century.

Your Safety Net Has Big Holes in It

Business is a game of strategies. First, you come up with a model for exchanging goods and services for a steady, predictable stream of cash. Next, you assemble the staff and automation tools that enable the maintenance of the revenue flow and expansion of activities to increase revenues and profit. If all goes as planned, you remain in business.

A major component of a business model is a set of contingencies that can be rapidly deployed if and when an event adversely influences the course of business. Contingencies are the keystone of a solid business strategy that cosigns responsibility for aspects of the model to other resources in case the expected outcome of the business model fails.

Say that goods sent to a customer are misdirected somehow by a common carrier. A contract between the customer and the common carrier shifts responsibility for the error to the common carrier who absorbs the loss. Cash flow remains uninterrupted.

A book publisher decides not to use capital to purchase printing equipment and instead contracts the manufacturing of the product to a vendor. Should the printing equipment fail or the printing plant be hit by labor problems, the book publisher exercises a contingency that invalidates the agreement with the printer, freeing the publisher to move manufacturing to another vendor. The original vendor is hit with the brunt of the problem while the book publisher experiences minimal if any impact on cash flow.

Contingencies are the safety net for industry. If contingency plans are properly incorporated into the business model, then the probability is slim that a catastrophic event will deliver a knockout blow to the business.

You probably have a safety net in place ready to provide you and your business with a fallback plan in case assumptions in the business model go astray. You should feel comfortable that your set of contingencies can handle practically any unforeseen problem. Are you sure that your safety net will save you from the year 2000 bug? Hold off from answering until you finish reading this chapter.

How Computer Systems Are Built

The lifeblood of business is the computer systems that manage daily operations and provide information to managers to help them navigate through the battlefield of competition. Typically a business has many computer systems. For example, an order entry system and accounting system are just two common systems that are found in most businesses.

The construction of the safety net for the company begins when the manager decides how mission critical systems are developed for the firm. The manager can decide to hire a staff of computer professionals and build the system internally. She can also employ temporary computer programmers called consultants to replace or enhance the capabilities of in-house staff.

For some systems, buying the software off the shelf is a more economical solution. A firm is foolish to hire a staff to create database software when large software manufacturers offer a more durable product for a relatively few dollars such as Oracle Access or Sybase.

Sophisticated systems like those that keep the books and records of the business cannot be purchased from the local software supermarket. Instead, a complete turnkey system that solves a particular business problem is purchased from a vendor.

A turnkey system, at times, must be modified to complement the way the firm operates. Here are three common approaches:

1. Pay the vendor to customize the vendor's turnkey system.

2. Purchase the source code from the vendor and have the in-house staff perform the customization.

3. Hire a consulting firm that specializes in building all or a portion of major systems to customize the turnkey system.

Another solution to automating a business is for businesses to outsource all of their systems. The systems are turned over to a vendor to maintain and support in exchange for an annual fee paid by the firm.

The decision of which method is used depends on the needs of management. Some managers want to retain control of every aspect of systems development and maintenance. Other managers find total control expensive, limiting, and risky. They would rather pay an annual fee and let someone else have all the responsibility for the system.

Simply, if the systems break down because of a bug—like the year 2000 bug—then the vendor is responsible for fixing the problem. If the problem cannot be fixed within a reasonable period, then the manager can drop the vendor and hire another vendor.

This flexibility provides a firm with a security blanket and protection against unforeseen risks involved with computer systems—or does it?

Safety Blanket for Staff-Built Software

Building a computer system in house seems like the safest way to protect the interests of the firm. You hire employees who have the expertise and are loyal to the firm. They are there to create software that meets the specific needs of your business. The firm owns the code, which can be modified at any time without any legal ramifications. What else could you ask for?

If I have just described the way your business approaches systems development, then are you in store for a shock when the stroke of midnight comes on December 31, 1999—if not before. That is the moment when your systems might think they are in January 1, 1900.

Here is what your firm faces:

- Current systems development projects will be placed on hold until your staff attacks the problem caused by the year 2000 bug.

- Expect that some of your more technical staff members will leave the project midstream to take advantage of the heavy demand for their talents—the ability to fix the year 2000 bug for firms that pay higher salaries than they are making with your firm.

- Prepare to accept full responsibility for correcting the problem.

Consider yourself on a sinking ship with your crew lowering the lifeboats rather than helping to plug the holes to keep the ship afloat. So what are your options? You cannot let the ship sink and there is no one coming to rescue you.

Here is what you need to do:

- Take action immediately. Remember, the clock is ticking.

- Prevent the exodus of your prime technical staff by negotiating better financial arrangements with them now.

- Offer them a contract that extends at least through the length of the project.

- Write into the contract a bonus that is only payable after the year 2000 bug fix is completed. This will give them an incentive to stay around until the project is completed.

- Attempt to add a clause to the contract that, if they should leave before the end of the project, they agree not to accept employment with a competitor or one of your vendors or customers.

- Avoid making promises to your technical staff that you cannot keep or have no intention of keeping. The staff has a good idea if your intentions are sincere and know where their career paths—if any—exist with your firm.

Staffing is just one of your concerns. You must overcome other obstacles such as inventorying your software and databases to make sure that you can find all of the programs so that they can be changed. You will also need to take steps to ensure that your project team does not lose focus on the project. Later in the book I will show you several good tools and techniques that will ease this process.

Take precautions that your staff will stick around during this crisis. Start the project off on the right foot with a good supply of tools. Turn your attention to your attorney!

Your firm has obligations to vendors and customers that could be breached if your computer systems are not year 2000 compliant. Your staff might make a valiant effort to fix the problem, but what happens to your firm if the deadline is missed?

Some of the horror stories told in the first chapter may affect your firm. Is your firm liable if your computer sent noncompliant data to a vendor or customer which caused damage to their computer system? Are you protected from collateral damages that could arise from this erroneous data being transferred by a vendor or customer to another firm?

These are events that will keep you up at night—especially New Year's Eve, 1999. Do not be too quick to bank on your business insurance policy to cover your losses. The year 2000 bug may not be covered. More on that later in this chapter.

Safety Blanket for Software Packages Purchased Off the Shelf

After reading the last section, you might be thanking yourself that you opted not to hire your own computer staff to build your systems. Buying software from your local computer software supermarket seems like the safest bet—or is it?

Many firms, including those who have in-house systems departments, purchase software products from Microsoft, Borland, Oracle, and smaller software manufacturers who offer solutions in a box. Most of these software packages are tools such as database management software and spreadsheets which are used by the nontechnical staff to manipulate information that is critical for making business decisions.

Most of us have become so secure in using these packages that little thought is given to the accuracy of the information these programs generate. Ask yourself this: When was the last time you double-checked the results of a calculation performed by one of these products? You review the data that you entered into the formula and make the assumption that the formula itself is correct, including those that use date calculations.

However, the year 2000 bug in a built-in function of an off-the-shelf product can be like a loose cannon rolling around the deck of a ship in a storm. You know something is wrong and has the potential to cause serious damage but you cannot do anything about it.

The damage that can be inflicted by the hidden bug can result in poor business decisions and have a collateral effect with vendors and customers. Your worries about software were not over when you purchased an off-the-shelf product. In fact, your troubles are just beginning. Here's what you can do:

- Review the warranty that is supplied with the product to determine exactly what the manufacturer warranties. You will be shocked to find that very little protection in this document is given to the customer. The warranty is designed to protect the manufacturer—not you.

- Avoid interpreting the warranty yourself, unless you have legal training. You are walking in a minefield where the knowledge of your corporate attorney is vital to your survival.

- The remedy for violation of the warranty is usually replacement of the software product.

- Software manufacturers normally excuse themselves from liability of collateral damage that may occur from the use of their products. This means if you are sued by a customer for providing wrong information that was generated by the off-the-shelf product, the software manufacturer is not liable. At least, according to the warranty. Your opinion and that of your attorney and the courts may differ.

Manufacturers of off-the-shelf software products that are not year 2000 compliant are not hiding the fact that the bug exists in their product.

Many of them are saying that the problem is industry wide and was known by the average customer when the product was purchased.

This fact, according the manufacturers, frees them of liability. The customer knew the bug existed in the industry; the customer did not inquire about whether or not the product was year 2000 compliant before the purchase was made; therefore, the customer assumed the risk by purchasing the product.

This thought does not give you much comfort. So what action can you take to rectify the problem and reclaim all or some of your losses? Here are some tips:

- Weigh the cost of litigation against your actual loss. Over the course of the case, legal fees can exceed the monetary loss caused by the year 2000 problem—even if you win the case.

- The main focus is to get the problem fixed, which can be difficult since you have no direct control over the manufacturer.

- Assess your clout with the manufacturer of the software. If you are a large customer, then you can exercise influence over the timeliness of the fix, especially now since the problem is not here yet (although it is imminent).

- If you have diminutive influence over the software manufacturer, then try to combine your efforts with those of other customers. Collectively, you will be able to get the attention of the manufacturer.

- Determine the viability of the manufacturer. Remember that the cost of repairing the year 2000 bug is not inexpensive. If the manufacturer is undercapitalized or expected sales volume for the product is not strong, then the manufacturer may walk away from the problem, and there is little that you and other customers can do to recover.

The Case of the Great Idea

You may find that the software company that developed your system does not have the resources to fix your problem. If the developer was a small company with few employees then it is likely that they may not be capable of paying for outside help to solve the problem. Larger developers may have more resources. However, these resources may be tapped if litigation becomes rampant. This phenomenon has not yet taken place and may never occur. It is wise to go to your developer, though, regardless of size and seek the help you need to solve your problem as soon as possible. If you wait, you may have to wait in line.

Safety Blanket for Vendor Software

A common practice among business managers is to buy a turnkey system from an outside vendor. The system is already built, tested, and used by similar businesses in the same industry. This is a very economical method of indirectly sharing resources. There is no need for each firm in the industry to reinvent the wheel.

There is security in knowing that the vendor's computer department is responsible for the development, support, and maintenance of a mission critical system. The business need only pay a one-time fee for the software and an annual support/maintenance fee.

If this sounds like your business systems, don't become too comfortable. You may be caught when the year 2000 bug comes out of hiding. The responsibility for ensuring that your mission critical system is ready for the twenty-first century lies with the vendor, not you. However, if the vendor fails to live up to this responsibility, your business is at risk and your hands could be tied in such a way that you can't legally fix the system yourself—even if you purchased the source code from the vendor.

Here are factors that may hamper your ability to fix the bug yourself:

- If you do not purchase the source code, then you have only an executable file that cannot be modified without having the source code.

- You can decompile—convert the executable file into source code—if you have the right tools to decompile, then recompile, the source code back to an executable file.

- Make sure your attorney reads your contract with the vendor to determine if you have the right to decompile and modify the source code yourself. Although you may be physically able to correct the bug, you may still need permission from the vendor to do so.

- Do not assume that warranties provided by the vendor protect your firm. Some vendors disclaim liability and claim the year 2000 bug constitutes assumed risk by your firm since the problem was well known in the industry when your firm purchased the system.

- You might find that fixing the year 2000 bug is outside the scope of your maintenance contract with the vendor.

Probably the most important point to remember is that you purchased the system. You own the system within the terms of the agreement, and the terms could be very similar to the terms when you purchased off-the-shelf software. That is, you did not purchase the source code. You purchased the license to use the software. All changes to the source code must be made at the discretion of the software manufacturer, not the customer.

Safety Blanket for Software Built by Temporary Employees

In an effort to reduce overhead, some firms hire temporary computer programmers to build their systems. The firm pays a consulting firm a premium daily amount for a relatively short period of time for an on-site programming staff to write the system.

After the system is tested and becomes part of a firm's operation, the temporary staff is terminated. Ongoing maintenance of the system is handled by a skeleton staff of employees and the firm avoids the overhead of maintaining a large, permanent staff of expensive programmers.

But what happens if your system is not year 2000 compliant? Who do you get to fix the problem? No one! Here are the problems that you face:

- You do not have a technical staff to address the problem.

- The consulting firm who supplied you with temporary programmers may not be able to find qualified programmers to work on your project. Those consulting firms, in many cases, are really a version of an employment agency for temporary workers. So the consulting firm is competing for a limited number of qualified programmers who know how to fix the problem. They may not be able to attract programmers for your project.

- There may be insufficient funds in your current budget to support the modification of your software.

- Unless you imposed standards when the system was built, the source code may not be easy to inventory and fix.

The full brunt of the liability for the problem lies with your firm. Normally, the consulting firm who supplied the programmers only guarantees that the programmers have the technical skills necessary to perform the job. If this later turns out not to be the case, the consulting firm does not get paid. However, the consulting firm is not liable for the system built by temporary employees.

If you find yourself in this situation, here are some steps that might help:

- Make sure that all temporary employees adhere to the standards that are in place for all systems that are built in house.

- Inventory all the source code immediately.

- Follow the recommendations I made to help you fix the year 2000 problem if you built the software in house.

Safety Blanket for Software Built by Computer Consulting Firms

A business that hires a consulting firm to build a computer system does so with the confidence that the responsibility for the system lies with the consulting firm. The business staff establishes the business rules, then turns the rest of the development over to the consulting firm who has a permanent, full-time staff that builds the system off premises.

When the system is completed, software is turned over to the business for testing and implementation. Support and maintenance of the system can lie with either the consulting firm or the business depending on the terms of the contract.

If your firm follows this option of building computer systems and you feel that the year 2000 problem is not your problem, think again! The responsibility for your system is clouded. Your firm has some responsibility, the consulting firm has some responsibility, and some responsibility is not clearly assigned.

Here are some points to consider:

- Examine the contract with the consulting firm to determine the lines of responsibilities.

- Determine if the consulting firm included any disclaimers. Typically the consulting firm warrants that the software will comply with the business rules established by the client. However, this excludes any performance problems that are caused by the client's equipment or by outside influences such as a virus. The year 2000 falls into the class of a virus, according to some consulting firms. Therefore, they are not responsible for fixing the problem free of charge.

- Examine the documents that contain the business rules that you provided to the consulting firm. If dates and date calculations exclude the century portion of the year, then the consulting firm could be in full compliance with the business rules and still not address the year 2000 bug.

- Determine if your staff contradicted terms of the contract and if their modifications invalidated any warranties provided for by the consulting firm.

Expect that there will not be an easy resolution of the conflict if you and the consulting firm disagree on responsibility for fixing the year 2000 bug. Both sides can bring in lawyers to fight for their position, but the bug still exists in your software—the mission critical system that is running your business—and of course the clock is ticking down.

Consider spending your energies addressing your problem and avoid becoming sidetracked over who must fix the problem. In the end, your business must still be alive in the year 2000.

The Case of the Changing Specifications

A company set out to create an inventory system where programs forecast the future levels of inventory based on historical data and current product demand. Management reviewed the various approaches available for building the system and decided to acquire a turnkey system and have the vendor modify the system according to the needs of the firm.

The contract called for the specification to be given to the vendor before work began on the project. This gave the vendor sufficient information to determine the scope of the changes and be able to give the client a firm price. Furthermore, the vendor wrote a clause that said once a change is requested after the original specifications were submitted in writing to the vendor, the contract was null and void. No one questioned this clause since the terms were reasonable. The vendor quoted a price based on a list of specifications submitted by the client. If the client imposed a new requirement, the expectation was that the quote would change and a new contract be issued.

As programming began on the project, managers who were not privy to the terms of the contract sent written requests for changes to the system to the vendor. The changes were prioritized on the work schedule with no mention of the effect the changes had on the contract.

Before work began on the new changes, the client inquired about whether or not the software was year 2000 compliant. It was not. The client then pointed to the maintenance agreement and other terms in the contract. These conditions seemed to obligate the vendor to fix the bug.

However, the vendor asked what contract the client was talking about. The vendor showed the letter that requested modifications in the system that were not part of the original specification list. The contract was void, according to terms agreed on by both parties.

The client had to renegotiate the contract and include terms that addressed the year 2000 bug. Of course, the new fee for the modifications reflected the cost of making the system year 2000 compliant.

....

Safety Blanket for Outsourced Systems

The trend in a number of industries is to outsource the entire information systems department to a firm who is prepared to manage the department and provide computer services for an annual fee. This option is favorable to companies who are looking to reduce the increasing cost of computer services.

As part of a typical outsourcing agreement, the outsourcing firm absorbs most if not all of the existing staff, computer systems, and in some cases computer hardware and facilities. This, like many of the options explored in this chapter for addressing systems needs, appears to be a way to shift the problems related to computer systems, including the year 2000 bug, to another firm.

In many cases, this objective is achieved, depending on the contract between the firms. The outsourcing firm knowingly agrees to take on all of the burdens of supporting and maintaining existing systems of the company, regardless of the condition of the systems.

However, you should consider certain factors before you pop the cork to welcome in the new century. Here are some of them:

- Review the outsourcing agreements immediately to determine if there is a clause that allows the outsourcing firm to charge above the annual fee to fix the year 2000 bug. This step is especially important if the outsourcing agreement was signed in recent years when the bug was known to exist.

- Pay careful attention to the clause that addresses fixing viruses, defects, and bugs that are found within the programs that are part of the outsourcing contract. This clause identifies responsibility for repairing normal problems within the existing code. However, this clause should also address the year 2000 bug.

- Look at sections of the outsourcing contract that define the size of the expected workload. If the workload exceeds expectations, then additional charges can be incurred. This is the section of the contract that may overrule the viruses, defects, and bugs clause mentioned above as this pertains to the year 2000 bug.

- If you are a value-added reseller, you must be certain that your suppliers are year 2000 compliant. This warranty needs to be written into the contract.

- Most of all, keep up to date on the financial stability of the outsourcing firm. The firm probably has more than one client and could find itself in a crunch for funds and resources fixing the year 2000 bug for all their clients within the same time frame. If the outsourcing firm fails to fix the problem, the mission critical systems that keep your firm afloat will stop. This remains your firm's problem.

Watch When Buying New Software

In the previous sections, I attempted to give you tips on how to address the year 2000 bug problem that exists in your current systems. You will find much more information on how to attack this problem in later chapters. However, your firm acquires new software every day, which gives you the opportunity to avoid software that is not compliant with the year 2000.

New software includes that purchased off the shelf and from turnkey systems from vendors and software that is encoded into chips on hardware that you purchase. When I mentioned hardware, you immediately thought I meant computer hardware, right? However, I also include the hardware that runs your elevator, telephones, climate controls in your buildings, and other pieces of equipment that contain small computers.

It is safe to say that there is a chance you will find a small computer in almost any sophisticated piece of equipment that you purchase, including watches, electronic diaries, and camcorders. Any piece of equipment that tracks time internally is a potential site for the year 2000 bug.

Before you purchase any software or hardware, send the manufacturer a letter asking if their software is year 2000 compliant. A negative response should obviously cause you to reject the product. However, there are times when this is not practical, especially in a limited market where only one or two products are available that meet your needs—and they are both not in compliance.

Manufacturers might respond by saying that the current version of their product is not year 2000 compliant. However, they are currently working on this problem and will upgrade their software at no charge when the problem is fixed. This statement should raise a caution flag in your mind. Will the firm be able to fix the problem before time runs out? Will the firm be around to deliver the upgrade? These are two important questions that must be raised in your assessment of the product.

The letter inquiring about compliance with the year 2000 is a protection of your rights. In some situations, failure to send a letter of inquiry before purchasing the software could be taken as a waiver of the manufacturer's responsibility to fix the problem without charge to you. This is even true if you have not made this inquiry in writing before entering into a maintenance contract with the manufacturer.

Furthermore, some insurers feel that this inadvertent waiver precludes your insurance company to subrogation against the manufacturer if the year 2000 bug causes an interruption of your business. Be sure to consult your attorney before you begin the purchasing process.

With all purchases of software and hardware that occur before the year 2000, you should require the manufacturer to provide you with a warranty that states the software is or will be year 2000 compliant. Furthermore, the warranty should provide indemnification for direct or collateral losses that occur for failure compliance with the warranty.

Any and all representations of performance of the product should be made part of either the contract with the manufacturer or the warranty. Failure to do this opens the door for a sales representative to verbally promise you that the product is in compliance. Later when the bug arrives and you bring up this fact to the manufacturer, all recollection of the sales representative's promise may be forgotten.

Do not be intimidated by preprinted contracts offered by manufacturers. These are purposely designed to prevent you from altering the terms that are most favorable to the manufacturer. Standard contracts can be modified.

Here are some guidelines to follow:

- Avoid purchasing software and equipment if the manufacturer refuses to put in writing that the product is year 2000 compliant.

- If you must make such a purchase, have your attorney negotiate a contract that requires the manufacturer to make the software compliant at the manufacturer's own expense. Also, there should be clear, financial penalties for noncompliance.

- Develop a contingency plan in case the manufacturer fails to make the product in compliance or goes out of business before the software is changed.

Is the Software and Hardware Supplier Still Around?

When a key vendor is unable to continue to supply a firm's needs, a cold fear sets in with management. Your dependable source of a mission critical supply is cut off suddenly and without warning. Further complicating the situation is that a long lead time could be necessary to find a replacement vendor, and during the search for a new vendor your business begins to flounder.

You might face this situation the first business day of the next century. Vendors who supply you with turnkey systems and hardware probably have seen most of the revenue that will be generated from your account. What revenue remains is in the form of a maintenance agreement, which is an insurance policy. The vendor is betting that your account will need little or no maintenance and you are betting that the cost of maintaining the system over time will cost more than the sum of the annual maintenance change.

Unless a disaster hits or a new version of the vendor's software or hardware is released, chances are that the vendor will win the bet. However, this is true under normal conditions. The year 2000 bug is atypical of the bugs or problems that are commonly found within programs. So the question that you must ask yourself is this: Is the vendor able to and willing to remain in business until the bug is fixed?

A vendor may make a sincere attempt to fix the problem, only to discover that there are insufficient financial resources available to complete the project. Furthermore, the vendor may evaluate the situation and decide that fixing the problem will have little if any short- or long-term positive effect on the vendor's bottom line. Simply, the product will remain marginally profitable after the cost of fixing the bug is taken into consideration. In such a case, it is better for the vendor to close up shop than to fix the problem.

In both scenarios, your firm loses regardless of whether you have or do not have an ongoing maintenance agreement with the vendor. Although you cannot prevent the collapse of the vendor unless your firm wants to lend financial resources, you can look for warning signs of forthcoming disaster. Keep in mind that the objective of this exercise is to identify a potentially lethal problem early so you can take evasive action. The key to avoiding being a victim of the year 2000 bug is having sufficient time to correct the problem. The surest way of becoming a victim is to assume the fix of the year 2000 bug is the vendor's problem. Legally you may be correct; however, practically your firm is the one being penalized.

Here are some factors to consider when analyzing your vendors:

- Assess the annual revenue flow the product provides to the vendor. Some products are at the end of their life cycle and leave little incentive for a vendor to make a sizable investment fixing the product.

- Determine if ownership of the product has changed recently. Some vendors who have no intention of fixing a product transfer ownership of the product to a new subsidiary corporation in an effort to isolate the parent company from product liability suits. The only asset of the subsidiary corporation is the product, so if you bring suit against the subsidiary because the firm failed to fix the year 2000 bug, you might end up owning the problematic software yourself. All the financial assets are with the parent corporation, not the subsidiary.

- Watch out for the forced upgrade. The maintenance agreement with the vendor might bind the vendor to fix the year 2000 bug and the product is still profitable so abandonment is out of the question. A vendor might tell customers that work is progressing on the fix, however, most of their effort is in building a "new" product. Of course, the "new" product is year 2000 compliant. In essence, the vendor enhanced the existing product, then called it a new product. The difference in these terms means that the expensive fix—one of the enhancements—is passed along to the customer and the fix of the existing system falls way behind schedule. The only logical choice is for customers to buy the new and improved version.

The Fine Print

It is safe to say that vendors and their customers have a mutually dependent arrangement. Both need each other to continue business operations. The rules that govern with arrangements fall into two categories: those that are verbal and those that are within a contract. Verbal rules are used during the day-to-day relationship and have little or no impact on the long-term arrangement, which is governed by contractual terms.

When times become tough, such as financing the cost of fixing the year 2000 bug, vendors and clients refer to the language contained in their written agreement. Your lawyer can advise you on terms of the contract. However, there are a few fine points in a contract that you need to review with your attorney.

I have discussed previously in this chapter many of the details that are in a contract with your vendor. In addition to revisiting these areas with your attorney, you must also concern yourself with a typical clause in a contract called "force majeure." In English, a *force majeure* clause means that you cannot take action against a vendor for software that does not work because of an Act of God.

Normally, nonperformance of material terms of the contract are grounds for breach of contract, which gives you the option to seek legal remedies or simply terminate the contract. An exception to this rule is if nonperformance is caused by an Act of God, which is outside the control of the vendor.

The question that must be answered is whether or not the year 2000 bug is considered an Act of God and beyond the reasonable control of the vendor. Some attorneys feel that the year 2000 bug is not an Act of God. Instead they feel that the problem is known and can be fixed if the vendor takes the proper steps to correct the problem.

However, other attorneys differ with this opinion and suggest that the deciding factor of whether or not a vendor can impose the *force majeure* clause as a defense for not fixing the year 2000 bug before the turn of the century is determined by the language of the clause. If worded incorrectly, then the vendor can walk away from the problem, leaving your firm without recourse.

Another critical aspect of a typical vendor contract is a clause that voids the vendor's warranty or other promises made to you. A key provision is that only the vendor or the vendor's designee is permitted to modify the system. If someone other than the vendor touches the code, then the vendor has the option to refuse to maintain the software or be responsible for any nonperformance of the software.

Keep this clause in mind if time is growing short and there is no sign that the year 2000 problem is being fixed by the vendor. There is a natural tendency for a manager to take matters into her own hands and cause the system to be modified without the knowledge or permission of the vendor. Any current or future problems with the system become the responsibility of the customer in such a case.

This factor is also true if changes were made by you to the software for problems that did not relate to the year 2000 bug. Say that your staff added a field to a database without the permission of the vendor. This change could free the vendor from correcting the year 2000 bug because your staff violated the terms of the original contract.

Virus Versus Bug

Is the Year 2000 Problem a bug or a virus? The answer to this question could determine whether or not a vendor is responsible for repairing the software at no cost to you. A *virus* is commonly defined as a program that is designed to be destructive to software on your computer. A *bug* is an error in the logic of the program. Simply, a bug is a defect in the program that causes the program to fail to operate properly.

Keep in mind that these are definitions that pigeonhole the year 2000 bug as a bug and not a virus. However, the definition used by your vendor may reclassify the bug as a virus. Whether the problem is called a virus or a bug does not matter. The system simply does not work.

It does matter how a vendor classifies the year 2000 bug. Some vendor contracts exclude the vendor from the responsibility of correcting problems that are caused by a virus. A virus on board a computer's hard disk is a sign of lack of precautions taken by the customer and has nothing to do with the logic and the coding used in the vendor's software. The vendor's software works fine; however, due to a lapse of security by the customer, a virus entered the computer and prevented the system from operating.

Here are some arguments to make if the vendor tries to define of the year 2000 bug as a virus:

1. Is the problem caused by another program that entered the customer's computer?

2. Do other customers of the vendor's have the same problem with the vendor's software?

3. Is there a direct link among the vendor's customers' computers?

If the answers to questions 1 and 3 are no and question 2 yes, then in all likelihood the problem is not caused by a virus. The problem is a fault with the logic of the program that is totally under the vendor's control and should be fixed at the vendor's expense depending on the terms of the purchase contract.

The Problem Is with Their Program

Your business is not operated in a vacuum. You have business partners such as vendors and customers that you must communicate with daily. Much of this communication takes place with the computer over the telephone lines. Data from one computer is transmitted to your computer so that your files can be updated as is the case with electronic bank reconciliation.

The accuracy of the data generated by your computer system is often dependent on the accuracy of those systems that transmit information to you. This adds another level of complexity when addressing the year 2000 bug. Now your firm must be concerned that your systems are updated as well as those of your business partners. Disaster can strike if all the systems are not operating properly.

How do you know if your systems will stop running even if you spend time and money to fix the year 2000 problem? The only way to answer this question is to make sure that your team considers your systems and those systems that feed your systems data, as well as systems that receive data from your system. The key here is to test by simulating dates into the next century.

Here's where to begin:

- Make sure your staff follows the flow of data that enters and leaves your business.

- Draw a flowchart that shows the processing of each feed and the source of the data.

- Contact your business partners and determine if and when they plan to have their systems year 2000 compliant.

- Monitor the progress of both your year 2000 project and that of your business partners to ensure that each one is on schedule for meeting the deadline. Keep in mind that your systems and those of your business partners must all be compliant by midnight December 31, 1999. If any one system is not, then all of the systems could fail.

Before Your Try to Fix the Problem Yourself...

Hopefully by now you have a pretty good understanding of the year 2000 problem. If you are aggressive, you are planning to meet this challenge head on. Roll up your sleeves, assemble a crackerjack team of managers and technicians, and start fixing the problem yourself.

Wait! Before you take this approach, you still have research to do—legal research. You may be physically able to correct your software but there could be serious legal hurdles that will hold you back. Let's discuss a few points to discuss with your attorney before having your team delve into your systems.

There is a copyright on the software used to run your business. If your firm built the software from scratch, then your firm holds the copyright and has the right to modify the software at will. However, you may not have this right if the software came from someplace outside your firm.

Begin your research by taking inventory of all the software used in your business and determining how the software was acquired by your business. Locate all purchase agreements, licenses, and warranties for the software. These will help you and your attorney determine if you retain the right to modify the program—and the repercussions if you do so.

You might learn that you do have the right to fix the year 2000 bug yourself. However, in doing so, you release the vendor from all liability for anything that goes wrong when running the software. This might be a heavy price to pay for doing something that keeps your business afloat.

The copyright applies to run-time versions of the software and to the source code. So just because you purchased the source code for a product does not mean that you automatically acquired the rights to change the program. You have to be given this right explicitly from the author of the software, otherwise you can open yourself up to legal action.

Firms that have access to the source code of a program that was written outside the firm can be tempted to create a new program using all or part of the current source code. Avoid this temptation unless your attorney advises you that you do have the right to proceed. Federal copyright law protects the author's current version of the software and derivatives of the work. So the new software that you plan to create is really a derivative of the current software and is covered under the copyright.

A copyright remains in effect for the life of the author plus 50 years. If the owner of the copyright is a corporation, then the copyright is in effect for 75 years. This only applies to software developed since 1978. Check with your attorney for more information about software created prior to 1978.

Who holds the copyright to the software that you use in your business? The answer depends on several factors. If the software was purchased off the shelf or as a turnkey system from a vendor, then chances are that you do not own the copyright. The software manufacturer or vendor owns the copyright.

However, if you hire employees, temporary employees, or a consultant to build the software, then chances are you own the copyright to the software. The software is considered work for hire when the software is built during the normal scope of regular employment. As a precaution, make sure that anyone hired by you to write software explicitly signs a waiver to ownership of the software.

An avenue that some attorneys see as a way to break through the copyright protection at least sufficiently enough to fix the year 2000 bug is with the concept of "essential step." This concept states that you may make changes in the program if those changes are an essential step in using the program. Simply, you might be able to make modifications as needed to make the software run properly on your computer. On January 1, 2000, the program will not operate on your computer unless you make the necessary modifications to the problem. Check with your attorney to determine if this is a valid approach in your state.

Other avenues to provide limited relief from copyright protection are fair use doctrine, the first sale doctrine, and the private use doctrine. The fair use doctrine states that you can infringe on an author's copyright based on the circumstances of how you use the software. This involves:

- The purpose for which the software is used;
- The nature of the software itself;
- The depth of the infringement; and
- The effect the infringement has on the market for the software.

Simply, if your infringement is just enough to keep the software running your business, then you may be allowed to violate the author's copyright based on the fair use doctrine.

The first sale doctrine states that after the author sells the copy of the software to you, the author's rights are terminated as to just that single copy of the software. Simply, the author has been rewarded for her work and now you can modify your copy of the program without violating the author's copyright.

The private use doctrine gives protection to you as long as the changed program is for your use only. That is, you cannot sell your corrected version on the open market.

Consult your attorney before starting any modification of software to which you may not own the copyright.

Going Offshore to Fix the Problem

Expect a shortage of qualified programmers who can fix your programs so that they work in the new century. Every business and government agency is looking for the same technicians. Faced with this reality, some managers are looking to ship the work abroad to countries like India where there are qualified programmers.

Arrangements are usually made within the United States with consulting firms based abroad. Terms can call for a copy of the software to be electronically transferred outside of the United States. Another method of achieving the same result is for the foreign firm to be given direct access to the client's computer via telephone lines and, at times, by using the Internet. In this case, the software and the work in progress never leave the client's computer.

By now you can imagine that there are factors you must consider before you agree to have the year 2000 bug fix abroad. At the top of the list of factors is the export rules imposed by the federal government. Software that you use in your firm may encrypt data to protect the information as the data is transferred over public telephone lines with business partners.

However, the Arms Export Control Act places some encryption software on the U.S. Munitions List and thus it is prohibited from being exported from the United States. This means that you could be prevented by the Office of Defense Trade Controls of the Department of State from allowing your software to be worked on outside the United States as long as the encryption program is part of your program.

Consult the Office of Defense Trade Controls before you make arrangements with firms outside of the country. You are probably required to apply for an export license from the Department of Commerce and you may need the permission of the National Security Agency before any software leaves the country or is worked on your computer via an international telephone connection.

Firms that have programming work performed overseas find that there is a wealth of experienced programmers especially knowledgeable in COBOL out there. Many mainframe legacy systems are written in COBOL and the offshore services are less expensive than those of similar firms within the United States. So, if you can overcome any export restrictions and you need to have a large amount of code fixed in the shortest possible time, then explore programming services in the Philippines and India.

The Hurdle of Decompiling Executable Programs

The only way the year 2000 bug can be fixed in your programs is if your staff can find the source code for those programs.

Earlier in this book I pointed out that one of the major obstacles facing many businesses and government agencies is that no one on your technical staff may know where the source code is for your legacy systems. Your legacy systems run perfectly for decades and the responsibility for those systems has changed hands more than tenfold times. The programmer currently responsible for those systems prays that no one asks for any changes.

Now the time has come for changes and, after the shock has worn off of learning that the source code is lost, you are still left with no source to change. The technical solution is to decompile the computer-readable copy of your systems into source code. Once this is completed, you have the new copy of the source code and your technical staff can make the fix. The new copy of the source code will then compile the source code back into computer-readable code.

However, do not be too quick to proceed with this operation. Throughout this chapter I have highlighted the many legal stumbling blocks that are in your way to modify programs to make them year 2000 compliant. The decompiling process too may violate federal and contractual law.

First, if your firm built the systems from scratch, then you are free to decomplile and make the necessary changes. You own the programs. However, if the systems came into your firm in any other way, then contact your attorney before calling your computer programmers.

Vendors commonly only supply customers with executable versions of their systems. The customer has the license to use the vendor's software and not the right to modify the software. The vendor holds the copyright to the product and therefore has the only right to decompile the run-time version of the system into source code.

Of course, what happens if the vendor refuses or cannot modify the system in time for the turn of the century? As suggested in previous sections, you may retain the right under the exclusionary doctrines in the copyright law to decompile the run-time version of the system.

Sending Your Software Out to be Fixed

The reality of making your mission critical systems year 2000 compliant is that you probably do not have enough staff members to fix the problem in all your programs. If you are like many firms, the practical solution is to send the software to an outside computer programming firm to fix the problem. On the surface, this seems the only practical solution. Your technical staff handles the daily routine and the consulting firm handles the once-in-a-lifetime problem.

Stop! Call in the lawyers to read the fine print in your agreement with vendors to determine if you are permitted to have a third party fix your system. This, of course, assumes that you have the right to make the fix yourself. Your contract with the vendor may prohibit you from showing the system and especially the source code to a third party. The basis of this clause is confidentiality.

Some vendors consider the source code to their systems to be a trade secret. You purchase the right to use—not necessarily see—this secret when you are licensed to use their software. However, there is no agreement between the vendor and the third party who is fixing your software. Your firm may not have the authorization to let a third party decompile the run-time version of the vendor's software and look at the vendor's trade secrets.

Furthermore, some attorneys believe that making a copy of the executable version of the vendor's software and placing that copy on your computer so that a third party can decompile the programs infringes on the vendor's copyright. This may also breach your license agreement with the vendor.

As more firms are faced with calling in a third party to fix their systems, you can expect the issue about infringement of the vendor's rights to be flushed out by the industry and the courts. So it is critical that you explore with your attorney your rights to assign a third party to fix the year 2000 bug.

Must Your Share Holders Know of Your Problem?

For many public firms, the impact of the year 2000 bug on their business is severe. That is, the business is in jeopardy if the problem is not fixed in time. The nature of this problem might require that you disclose the situation to your shareholders.

The Generally Accepted Accounting Principles (GAAP) set forth by the American Institute of Certified Public Accountants require that circumstances involving uncertainty of possible gain or loss for the business must be disclosed in the financial statements of the firm. Some accountants feel that if the year 2000 bug can cripple your computer systems, then you must make this known as a note in your audited financial statements.

This notice must be reported in the body of the statement if you feel that it is likely that you will not fix the problem in time and that you cannot estimate the cost of the loss that will result. If losses can be estimated, then the loss might need to be charged against earnings.

Assessment of the potential damage to your firm may not be under your control. Your outside auditors will be obligated to review your plans for bringing your systems in compliance. Your auditor must conform to the Generally Accepted Auditing Standards (GAAS). This rule requires auditors to detect and report errors and irregularities that could be construed as intentionally false or misleading statements in a firm's financial statements.

Your auditor must determine your firm's ability to continue in business for a year and determine the effect, if any, the year 2000 bug will have on business operations. After reviewing your firm, the auditor may recommend that your company take steps to bring your systems up to date. Failure to do so could require the auditor to qualify her certification that the financial statements are representative of the firm's financial condition. This qualification paragraph must appear as part of the financial statement.

In addition to having to deal with your independent auditor's concerns, you must also consider the requirements of the Securities and Exchange Commission. All annual and quarterly reports must include a section where management discusses and analyzes material events and uncertainties that would affect the future financial condition of the firm.

If your firm's systems will be affected by the year 2000 bug, then you should consult your attorney about whether or not this fact must be reported to the Securities and Exchange Commission. Your firm would not be required to make such facts known if you feel either the fix of the year 2000 bug will be made before the turn of the century or that if the repair is not made, the repercussions will not affect the operating results of the firm.

Your firm is also under a similar obligation if the firm is about to offer shares to the public. Every registration statement of securities, including the prospectus, must reveal the negative effect of the year 2000 bug on the performance of the company, if one exists.

Failure to adequately disclose the disastrous effect the year 2000 bug could have on your company can open the firm up to lawsuits brought by shareholders. Furthermore, those officers of the firm who signed the financial and registration statements and all the directors of the firm (even if they did not sign) can be held liable for not revealing the potential problem.

Your problem may not rest solely with the shareholders. The Securities and Exchange Commission can investigate and assess penalties. Of course, failure to disclose conditions that could negatively impact your business might violate securities laws in one or more of the 50 states.

Before you become overly concerned about your liability, the statements must be known to be false at the time they are issued. If the statements are made in good faith, then the burden falls on the investor to perform due diligence before making a purchase. That is, the investor must ask relevant questions before buying the security.

Keep Creditors Informed

I talked about the need to inform your stockholders about the potential effect the year 2000 bug will have on your firm. You also need to inform your creditors about the potential problem. If your firm is like most, your company has credit lines with lenders and outstanding bank loans. The repayment of this debt depends on a steady cash flow of business—a cash flow that could be interrupted at the beginning of the century.

Credit is extended based on the current financial strength of your company and the continuance of that strength during the life of the debt. Any material changes in that premise could affect the terms of the loan and whether or not the lender is willing to continue accepting the risk. If your computer systems are not year 2000 compliant or will not be by the end of the century, then the basis for outstanding loans has materially changed.

Be prepared to undergo a review of your business by creditors soon. Many creditors will not wait for their debtors to voluntarily disclose the condition of their computer systems. Instead, they are expected to begin a very procedural review of their loan portfolio and determine if and where there is any unnecessary exposure.

Your firm should take the lead and not wait until your creditors begin their investigation. Here is what you should do:

- Begin with your own assessment of the impact of the potential problem on your firm.
- Determine if your plans for fixing the problem are realistic and will achieve the desired results on time.
- Contact your creditors and present your situation to them.
- Attempt to elicit their support. Remember, this is the time when you need a replacement for the normal cash flow that is generated by your business—and only your lenders are in a position to provide this source of cash.

Your forthrightness coupled with a good credit history, a long relationship with your creditors, and a solid plan for fixing the problem should be enough evidence to persuade your creditors to continue their support.

However, you cannot expect support from creditors if the realities of your situation and the impact to your business is not favorable. Banks must develop a clear picture of their loan portfolio so they can make any necessary adjustments to write-offs for expected defaults. You can expect bank records to be reviewed by bank examiners to determine if the bank adequately accounted for the impact of the year 2000 bug on their business.

Vendors' Strategies

Expect that vendors who supply your firm with software will not be aggressive in making their products year 2000 compliant unless there is a clear economic advantage for them to do so. Ideally, vendors like to pass along the cost of the update to customers directly. The only exception is if the vendor is in the process of enhancing their product with other features and the year 2000 bug fix becomes one of these enhancements.

Vendors protect themselves from unnecessary expense in maintaining their products by writing clauses into their licensing and maintenance agreements with their customers and within the warranty for their products.

Typically, vendors limit their liability by inserting a disclaimer in these legal documents. By either signing the contract or opening the sealed software package, your firm might have agreed to these disclaimers.

In addition to the use of disclaimers, vendors frequently specify the damages that they are liable for if terms of the contract, license, or warranty are breached by the vendor. It is not unusual for damages to be limited to the replacement or repair of the software. Rarely will vendors agree to be responsible for direct or collateral damages that arise out of their software's failure to operate properly.

The concerns that you and your legal counsel should have is whether the courts will uphold such clauses and liability limitations. Some attorneys feel that as long as these terms were agreed to by both parties, the courts will not overrule the terms of the agreement. Simply put, if your firm signed the agreement, then the terms are probably binding.

However, some attorneys raise the question of whether or not you are bound by a licensing agreement that the vendor attaches to the outside of the software package. According to the vendor, once you open the shrink wrap on the package, you have accepted the terms of the licensing agreement. Be sure to ask your attorney for an opinion.

Another issue is whether or not the disclaimers contained in the agreement with the vendor will protect the vendor from legal action based on product liability law and fraud. Unless the vendor explicitly states that the software is not year 2000 compliant, some attorneys feel that the vendor remains liable since a material defect in their product was not made known when the product was sold to you.

In such a case, the statutes of fraud and product liability laws might take effect, which allows you to seek direct and collateral damages from the vendor for losses caused by the vendor's software. Furthermore, there could be an implied warranty violation since the product is not performing as stated by the vendor at the time of the sale.

Vendors who build software for your firm might attempt to restrict their professional malpractice liability. We associate malpractice with medicine and law; however, some attorneys belief that professionals in various areas—including programming—are held to higher standards than a typical vendor. Therefore, in theory, the malpractice statutes could apply. Your attorney can research cases to determine if the courts agree with this theory.

Business Insurance

Throughout this chapter I have reviewed the many protection plans that are found in a typical business—all of which have big enough holes in them that they probably will not provide protection from the year 2000 bug. There is one kind of protection plan that I have not touched on until now. This is business insurance.

Business insurance is the ultimate protection for business liability. If all else fails, then your insurance carrier is there to provide financial resources to help you recover from the loss. The question that you must answer is will your current business insurance policy cover losses that occur due to the effect of the year 2000 bug on your business systems?

The answer depends on the kind of insurance that you feel should protect you. Generally, business insurance falls into two broad categories: policies that cover you if someone sues you, and policies that help you recover from an interruption in your business.

Liability insurance policies may protect your firm if errors caused by your computer systems negatively affect your business partners. However, before you can feel at ease, have your attorney review the fine print in your liability insurance coverage.

Business interruption insurance is a different consideration. Many policies require the interruption to be caused by a *fortuitous event*. Courts have defined this as an event that has occurred by chance based on the knowledge of the insurance carrier and of management of your firm.

If you find this clause in your business interruption policy, then be prepared for your insurance carrier to claim that interruptions caused by the year 2000 problem are not covered by the policy. The basis for this claim is that the year 2000 problem is not caused by chance but instead the problem was known of and there was a very high likelihood that the problem will interrupt business operations.

Since there is a possibility that your firm is not covered for business interruptions by your insurance carrier, you may want to contact your insurance carrier and ask for an explicit decision. This will give you time to react in case the decision goes against your firm.

Start Addressing the Problem

By now you realize that a serious problem could affect your computer systems in a few years, a problem that could jeopardize your business, expose your firm to potential liabilities, and create an unlimited number of headaches.

For the moment, time is on your side—but not for long. Unless you begin to address this problem immediately, your firm will not be able to sidestep the year 2000 bug. The bug may occur while your staff is still trying to make the necessary changes to your systems to prevent the bug from occurring—a frightening thought. For most teams of software engineers, it is not unusual to miss deadlines by three or more months. This is one that can't be missed.

If your firm is like most companies, there is no plan under way. No one has attempted to investigate the highly likely possibility that your systems will stop running properly at the stroke of midnight on December 31, 1999.

The clock ticks away daily toward this deadline—a deadline that you cannot move.

Even if your firm realizes this potential hazard, has anyone started to do anything serious about it? The problem can be monumental, one that practically no systems department has ever had to face. It's possible that none of your staff has the training to address the problem.

Avoid panic. In this chapter, I explore a logical approach to addressing the year 2000 problem. These suggestions will give you and your systems staff a starting point and guidelines to follow throughout this long and delicate project.

By the end of this chapter you will have a solid foundation with which to begin to develop your own plans for making sure that your firm can withstand the twenty-first century and dodge the mother of all computer bugs.

Where to Begin

You and your staff must understand that this is not the kind of project that you attack by the seat of your pants. It is so easy to fall into the trap of minimizing the scope of the project, especially for seasoned systems managers and programmers.

When you first heard about the bug, you were probably puzzled. You investigated the problem and discovered that your computer programs were about to subtract 99 from 00 and report wrong date-sensitive information. This did not seem like an earth-shattering problem. You were sure that you or your systems department could come up with a solution in a matter of weeks. But by reading the first two chapters of this book you see that this simple math error could bring down your firm, those of your business partners, and possibly the economy.

Now is the time for everyone who works on computers to address this problem. This includes the systems department as well as top management of your firm. If you are an independent contractor or self employed, it is critical that you take appropriate action. All must be convinced that the project that is about to be undertaken is a lifesaving mission and all red tape and politics in the firm must be placed aside until all the fixes are in production.

Once everyone is committed to the project, you must assemble a team of managers from all areas of the firm who work well with each other and have complimentary skills. This team must have full responsibility for reassigning and acquiring the resources that are necessary to address the problem.

Since this is a very broad scope of authority, team members must be high-level managers from the firm's finance and accounting, legal and systems departments, the chief administrator, and chief operating officers. These are the people who collectively can focus on an aspect of the problem, then do whatever is necessary to resolve the problem without having to restate the problem and their recommendations for action before approval is given.

The team must follow a formal methodology for approaching this problem. Failure to do so could cause the team to overlook serious trouble areas and therefore leave them in need of repair after the systems are placed into production.

Here are the steps that I recommend following:

- Organize a team whose members are authorized to make immediate and binding decisions.
- Inventory all your systems including those that are not obvious such as the software that runs your elevators and security systems.
- Assess the potential damage. Determine the extent to which each system is affected by the year 2000 bug. Identify the dependencies of each system including those that interface with business partners.
- Prioritize the work that must be performed on each system. Those mission critical systems that are impacted by the bug are the first that need to be addressed.
- Develop a timetable laying out when each system must be repaired, replaced, or deposed. Remember that more than one system will be worked on at the same time.
- Determine the resources that are necessary to get the job done on time.
- Estimate the cost of the repair and the source of revenue for the project.

- Develop a work plan that clearly assigns responsibility for each repair and develop or procure tools for monitoring progress.

- Create a solid testing plan to ensure that all of the systems, once repaired, operate perfectly in the production environment.

- Develop an implementation plan so that there is a smooth transition from the existing bug-riddled systems to the new bug-free system.

- Plan contingencies in case some or all of the systems are not in production in time for the new century.

The Case of…The Taxing Assessment

The administrators at a Chicago-based retail chain recently began assessing the impact that the year 2000 bug will have on their firm. They held off from defining strategies for addressing the problem. Instead, they set out to make a careful assessment of the situation.

The assessment process was tedious since theirs was a mixture of old and new software some of which was built in house and was either poorly documented or undocumented. Their hardware was not in any better shape. The firm used a mixture of technologies, some of which were no longer made.

About 45 full-time staff members were devoted to the assessment with the help of department specialists when they were required. They discovered that many of the systems that kept the firm in business had been around since 1982. Key systems were written in OS/VS COBOL and the data was stored in VSAM files within the MVS environment.

The firm's year 2000 team found that dates displayed on the screen and in reports could remain unchanged. Although only two digits were used to represent the year, all the staff who read the screens and reports knew that 00 meant the year 2000.

Furthermore, they planned to expand the date fields in databases to accept four digits instead of the current two digits. Small programs called *bridge programs* were going to be written to convert the date formats in routines that used date calculations. The conversion would take place right before the system performed the calculation.

To ease the impact of the change to the computer department, the year 2000 team proposed to make these modifications during normal maintenance of the system where possible.

The issue about using consultants, vendors, and offshore consultants on the project was easily decided by the year 2000 team. The firm had already explored the use of these services in normal business and developed a policy which set down who, when, and how such services could be employed by the firm.

The Scope of the Problem

The year 2000 bug will affect a vast array of computer software and hardware, some of which will not readily come to mind. The obvious areas to review are systems that affect mainframes, minicomputers, and personal computers. The less obvious are computer networks and telephone networks. Networks too have internal clocks and software that is used to operate network routers.

Other easily overlooked aspects of the problem are the programming languages used to write the systems in your firm. The obvious languages are COBOL, FORTRAN, SQL, C, and C++. The less obvious programming languages include BAL, PL/1, JOVIAL, and Pascal. There are two serious problems with systems written in these languages.

First, the systems in question are usually legacy systems written in the popular language of the day. Today these languages may be nearly obscure with few skilled programmers available. Simply said, you may not be able to find the technicians who know how to read and write in these older computer languages.

The next problem with these systems is that the programmers who wrote them probably did not conform to any standard style for writing structured code. This means that there may be little or no documentation for these systems and following the logic in the problem can become time consuming.

Let us explore another misconception about fixing the year 2000 problem. Some managers compare repairing the problem with the word processor feature of search and replace. Simply, load each program into an editor, then search for anywhere there is a date mask of YY. Once found, replace this mask with YYYY.

This approach seems logical, but in reality it is flawed! The date could exist in two places: in the database and in the programs that make up your system. The search and replace technique might work with the source code for the programs—assuming the source code and the search criteria (YY) were used in the program. But, keep in mind that throughout the investigation, you cannot make any assumptions.

The database poses another problem. The search and replace technique probably will not work since the names that are used to identify fields of the database are unique and may not conform to any naming convention. In a few systems you might find field names beginning with or ending with *dat* or *d* to signify that the value is a date. But even if such a convention is used, there is a good chance that the programmer did not use it for all the date fields. Naming conventions are left up to the programmer to enforce.

Another common way to identify dates within a database is to look at the data type of the field. Typically, fields that contain dates are identified as a date type. That is, only information in a valid date format is accepted into the field by the database management software.

However, the programmer could have also placed a date in a character field type. Since this too is a valid option for a programmer, you must physically look at the data inside each character field to determine if the information is a date and, if so, what format is used for the date. You must scan through large numbers of records to determine if the programmer was consistent in the use of the date format throughout the database.

Another obstacle that exists with databases is that they contain confidential information such as that used to consolidate financial records and personnel data. Field names in those databases could be encrypted to prevent anyone from knowing the contents of the fields. This means your programmer could search the field names of the database and be unable to recognize date fields unless a program is used to decode the field names.

A similar technique might have been used within these confidential programs to conceal the variables that are used to store critical dates. To make matters more complicated, some confidential systems do not use dates. Instead, date values are the result of a calculation encrypted into the program. Identifying these dates requires that your programmers know the following: that the date is an encrypted calculation; how to decode the calculation; and how to encrypt the calculation once the problem is fixed. Remember, these are date calculations in your legacy systems—systems written decades ago by programmers who are no longer around and who used tools (encryption software) that may no longer be supported by the manufacturer.

Dates or date calculations are used in a vast number of places in a typical system. Here are just a few dates used in a personnel system that is possibly the most common system used in most organizations today:

- Date hired;
- Birth date;
- Benefit enrollment date;
- Benefit eligibility date;
- Date assigned to a department;
- Date of next performance review; and
- Date terminated.

The year 2000 problem also lies in data that does not resemble a date, for instance, where the last two digits of the year are embedded into a serial number. At first glance you may say leave it alone. Everyone knows that the digits 00 mean the year 2000. That is fine for humans, but your computer will assume that a serial number with 00 year digits is for a product produced early in the twentieth century. This will become evident when the serial number is used for sorting or in calculations.

The Case of…The Standard Date Routines

A large financial firm in Boston started their year 2000 project by inventorying their systems. The investigation revealed that there were 2500 instances in their systems where the date was used in a calculation. But each time the code was used, it called a routine to perform the actual calculation.

The technical staff breathed a sigh of relief; they didn't have to change and test the changes made to 2500 calculations because there was only one group of code performing all those calculations. The change needed to be made in only one place.

Upon further examination, however, the technical staff found there were 150 individual routines that calculated dates for the various systems of the firm. Each one was a modification of the original routine which they could not locate. It seemed that over the decades, programmers, many of them consultants, copied whatever existing date calculation routine they found in the system, and then modified the routine to meet their current needs.

There were 150 undocumented routines that performed unique date calculations. Although this reduced the number of modifications to 150 rather than the original 2500 that the staff expected to change, the staff preferred to handle 2500 changes since the 150 routines actually made the task more complex. Each of the 150 routines needed to be fixed. Once fixed, the staff had to locate every line of code that called the routine. Finally, each of the 2500 lines needed to be tested to determine if the modification worked or caused further complications.

Compounding the problem was the fact that the date routines were written in BAL. This meant the firm had to locate consultants who knew how to read and write BAL, and very few were available. As of this writing, the work continues with great expectations that all the systems will be in working order come the first business day of the new century.

Inventory Hardware and Software

By now you should realize that the problem is more complicated than it may have appeared at first glance. Once you have organized your year 2000 team, the clock starts ticking and the game begins.

Begin by identifying everything in your firm that uses dates or could possibly use dates. Remember, some devices such as your building security system or your voice mail system do not normally come to mind when you mention the year 2000 problem.

Once identified, divide the work up into logical groups. These should include:

- Mainframe systems and hardware;
- Minicomputer systems and hardware;
- Workstations systems and hardware;
- Personal computer systems and hardware;
- Computer networks;
- Private telephone network and equipment; and
- Building services equipment.

One team for each group should be formed. Each team must have technicians who are familiar with the hardware and software used in each group so they can conduct an inventory of it. There should also be a documentation person who will have the responsibility for assembling the inventory records according to a standard style. There must also be one person to serve as group leader. This individual need not be a technician, just a good facilitator and decision maker.

The purpose of the inventory process is to gather information, not to decide whether or not a particular system or piece of hardware must be fixed, replaced, or discarded. This decision comes in the next step when a formal assessment is performed. It is critical for the inventory and assessment steps to remain separate, otherwise the teams conducting the inventory may easily lose focus and never complete the full inventory.

Inventory Method

The top-down approach is an excellent method to use when inventorying your firm. This approach requires the team to identify major systems and hardware first, then proceed to review the next level of each system and pieces of hardware until all the information necessary to complete the inventory is known.

Begin with your computer systems. Identify all the systems in your firm by

- Name;
- Platform;
- Programmer responsibility;
- Location on the platform;
- System creator;
- Importance of the system to your firm;
- Number of copies of the system and their location;
- Type of system.

Select one system and continue the inventory process. Now you are looking at the programs and databases that comprise the system. You need to identify the following:

- Name of the programs;
- Location of the programs;
- Function of each program;
- Name of the database;
- Location of the database;
- Name of the database management software manufacturer; and
- Name and location of compilers.

Continue with inventorying the details of programs and databases that are used by the system. Here is the information that you need to develop for each program and each database:

- Name and location of the executable code;
- Name and location of the object code;
- Name and location of the source code;
- Names and locations of libraries or shared code;
- Date information or date calculations if any;
- Name and location of screens used by the program;
- Name and location of tables in the database;
- Data dictionary of the tables;

- Name and location of indexes used in the database;

- Name of the fields used to create the key to the indexes;

- Location of any documentation; and

- Location of any locked or secured information about the systems.

A similar approach is used to inventory computer hardware. Develop the big picture first, then explore the details as the inventory process continues. Start with the following:

- Name and model of the hardware;

- Name of the manufacturer;

- Location of the hardware;

- Purpose of the hardware; and

- Staff member who is responsible for the hardware.

A more detailed look would elicit the following type of information:

- Hardware configuration;

- Hardware connections; and

- Any special equipment included inside the hardware.

Inventory Often Overlooked

Earlier in this chapter I mentioned items that are frequently overlooked during the inventory process. Since this is such an important area of the inventory, I think it wise to mention others so your team will not inadvertently miss them.

With computer hardware and software, you must make a record of those programs that are built by outside firms, many of which may be off-the-shelf packages. These include utilities programs and software tools used by technicians to build and maintain your systems and to keep your computer hardware operational.

Also included in this category are the operating systems that make your computers work. Most teams take the operating system for granted, but the operating system typically provides your programs with the current date and time. If the operating system is overlooked and it fails, most of your programs will fail too.

Any file on your computer should be included in the inventory regardless of whether the file appears important or not. As part of the detailed inventory, the team must review the contents of the file, if possible, to determine if the file includes a day and the association the file has with other systems.

You should not forget to review your firm's archived files. These are typically programs and data files that are periodically saved to tape, disk, or CD and stored off premises. Many times these backup files are totally forgotten by everyone except for the technicians who have the responsibility for maintaining the firm's archives. Only in cases of an emergency are these backup copies restored to the production system.

Of course, the restored programs and data files probably overwrite the existing programs and data files on the computer. This means unless changes are also made to the archived programs and data files, the year 2000 bug could find its way into your system at the worst possible time—in an emergency.

As part of the planning process you will decide if this data should be updated, replaced in part, or replaced in entirety. Inventorying may be more expensive than creating new archives to updated systems so you need to weigh the advantages and disadvantages. Remember that you do not want to hold on to programs or data that may still have the year 2000 bug.

Then there are those "noncomputers" that can potentially contain the bug. These include your voice mail system and electronic equipment such as your elevators, telephone system, and building security system. These too must be made part of your inventory.

Inventory Recordkeeping

The purpose of inventorying your software and hardware is to construct a record of all the possible areas of your firm that may be affected by the year 2000 bug. This record serves as the foundation for assessing the impact of the problem on your firm and the first step in developing a plan for addressing the problem.

Many styles of records are available that can be used to record your inventory. I suggest using two kinds of records: a leveling diagram and an inventory description. A *leveling diagram* is a flowchart showing the relationships among the systems. Each system and piece of hardware is represented as a symbol on the diagram. A symbol is typically a box that contains the name of the system or piece of hardware and a sequential number. The first box is 1, the next is 2, and so forth.

I stated that an approach to the inventory process is to begin at a high-level then work your way down to the details of each system and piece of hardware. Each level of detail can be depicted on a page of the leveling diagram and related to the previous high-level diagram by numbers that are assigned to the related symbols on the diagram.

Figure 4.1 contains a very abbreviated version of a high-level diagram of the inventory of systems in a typical firm. This diagram can obviously be expanded to include accounting systems and other systems that are found in your firm.

Each box in this diagram represents a system. The first box, numbered zero, signifies that the following boxes in the diagram represent components of a complete system. If this diagram is used to inventory hardware, then the name of the first box would be hardware.

Subsequent boxes symbolize systems in the firm. I used payroll, benefits, and order entry to illustrate this point. Each box contains a number used to identify the system uniquely and to relate the high-level diagram to the lower level diagrams.

Figure 4.1 *The highest level of a simple leveling diagram.*

Once all systems are identified on the high-level diagram, then you should create a lower level diagram for each system. One such diagram is shown in Figure 4.2. This illustration begins to inventory the components that make up the payroll system. Again, this is an abbreviated diagram. There are many more components of the system.

Each component addresses a particular function of the system. Each function, furthermore, contains a set of programs which contain the code that performs the related tasks. The user interface component is the programs and any databases that are used to gather information from the user and display information on the screen.

Notice that each of these boxes is also numbered. The number 1.0 in the first box indicates that payroll is the number 1 box on the high-level diagram and the first box (number 0) on this diagram. Likewise, the user interface is numbered 1.1 to indicate that this component is related to the payroll system.

Although I stopped at the second level diagram, you can expect the diagrams you create to proceed to further levels. Each level continues with the same number sequence. That is, the first program in the user interface component has the number 1.1.1.

Knowing the number of a box enables a technician to trace forward or back through various diagrams and determine how a particular box affects the entire firm. Furthermore, this technique reduces the confusion that is seen in many technical diagrams. The year 2000 team only needs to see the high-level diagram to help them create an overall plan for attacking the year 2000 problem.

In comparison, the project manager who is responsible for assuming the payroll system is in compliance need only review the midlevel diagrams that describe the payroll system. This is sufficient information for the project manager to assign programmers to investigate specific components of the payroll system.

The lower diagram of components of the payroll system is the perfect place for programmers to begin as they start to look at the code and at the related databases.

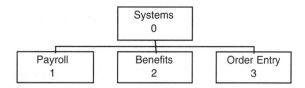

Figure 4.2 *This is the next level of detail for the payroll system.*

Leveling diagrams are a road map to your systems, and they are end products of the inventory process. Another end product of this process is the documentation of each piece that is being inventoried.

The mention of documentation conjures images of reams of unreadable text that even technicians avoid. This may be true in many cases, but it does not—and should not—be the end product of the inventory process.

The level diagram is the road map produced by the inventory process. The documentation produced by the same process is the travel guide. A travel guide provides you with key information and tips to help you on your trip. The road map shows you the way to get there. The combination of the two eases the anxiety of traveling.

Table 4.1 contains the kinds of information that should be included in the documentation. Some companies create a similar form which is completed by the inventory staff. The combination of the level diagrams and the documentation provides sufficient information for the year 2000 team to assess the problem.

You will notice that the information in Table 4.1 is directly related to a leveling diagram by the leveling diagram number—the number in a box on the diagram. In addition, the information is identified by two names; the first is the formal name for the piece of inventory and the second name—the acronym—is probably the name known more commonly throughout the firm.

A brief description of the functionality of the system must be included in the documentation. This should simply state the effect it has on the entire system.

Other information important for the inventory team to collect includes

- The name of the person currently responsible for the system;
- The last time changes were made;
- How the system or hardware was acquired; and
- What other systems depend on this system.

The last entry is critical to identify during the inventory process. The inventory team must identify the data storage areas (i.e., databases, tables, and indexes) and the flow of data into and out of the system. This information is necessary to ensure that any changes made will not adversely affect other systems. Likewise, you will know what systems must be changed; otherwise inconsistent data could be fed into your system.

After all the information shown on Table 4.1 is gathered and the leveling diagrams are completed, your year 2000 team has completed a significant portion of the task of ensuring that your systems will not fail because of the change in date. It is important to realize that although the information contained on this form is fairly detailed—and difficult at times to locate— you will need this information to perform the thorough assessment of your firm's situation. Now is not the time to take shortcuts and avoid the necessary grunt work. If you do, you will not enjoy New Year's Eve, 1999.

Leveling Diagram Number:

Name:

Acronym:

Function:

Technicians:

Last Upgrade:

Method Acquired:

Dependencies:

Database:

Tables:

Indexes:

Receives Data From:

Method Data Is Received:

Format Data Is Received:

Send Data To:

Method Data Is Sent:

Format Data Is Sent:

Location of Executable File:

Location of Object File:

Location of Source Code File:

Compiler:

Languages:

Vendor:

Location of Maintenance Agreement:

Maintenance Agreement Start Date:

Maintenance Agreement Termination Date:

Limitations That Prevent Fix:

Table 4.1 *Facts that should be included in the documentation.*

Who Should Conduct the Inventory

The inventory process provides the basis from which your firm can begin to address the problems caused by the year 2000 bug. Therefore, special consideration should be given to whomever conducts the inventory. Its a simple question that is complicated to answer. Here are the typical options:

- Current staff;
- Temporary staff; or
- An outside consulting firm.

There is no easy answer. Each option provides advantages and disadvantages, which are explored here.

Current Staff Advantages:

- Familiar with the systems and hardware.
- Have a mental history of recent changes to the system and hardware.

- Know the weaknesses of the system and hardware.

Current Staff Disadvantages:

- Chance that errors will remain uncovered to prevent repercussions to the staff who is responsible for the system or hardware.

- Overlooking key components because the staff is too familiar with the system or hardware.

- Lack of thoroughness because the staff assumes certain components will not be affected without reviewing the details of those components.

- Lack the expertise to fully inventory the systems or hardware and may be embarrassed to admit it.

- Must continue to support the current systems and hardware during the inventory process.

- May be reluctant to terminate existing systems or make unbiased judgments.

Temporary Staff Advantages:

- A fresh pair of eyes looking at components.

- Provide technical expertise not available with the current staff.

- Bring experience gained from fixing the year 2000 problem somewhere else.

- Frees nonsupervisory staff to continue to support the current systems and hardware.

Temporary Staff Disadvantages:

- Lack of impetus for doing a good job. They have no stake in the firm and receive the same rewards regardless of how the job is performed.

- Could be negatively influenced by the current staff who supervise the temporary staff. The supervisor might steer the temporary staff away from components that would negatively expose the supervisor as inefficient, incapable, etc.

- Underqualified temporary staff. Simply said, the firm can easily be told that the temporary staff has skills which they do not have. The firm then depends on an "expert" who does not have expertise.

Outside Consulting Firm Advantages:

- Fresh eyes looking over your systems and hardware.

- Bring their own supervision and staff.

- Frees both nonsupervisory and supervisory staff to continue to support current systems and hardware.

- The consulting firm seeks to perform a good job so they might be invited back to address other problems of your firm.

- Experience fixing the year 2000 problems for other firms.

Outside Consulting Firm Disadvantages:

- The consulting firm may sell its services, leaving an insufficient number of consultants to do the inventory in a timely fashion for your firm.

- The consulting firm may drop your firm or reduce its priority if they receive a request from a larger client.

- The consulting firm may send inexperienced consultants to perform the inventory. Major consulting firms are noted for hiring staff who have just graduated from college, then charging your firm the price of an experienced consultant.

- The consulting firm may not have all the experience that the salesperson claims the company has.

- Your firm's systems and hardware are shared with strangers who may be hired by your competitor.

Although you have some of the same advantages and disadvantages of the options experienced in staffing the inventory process, there does not seem to be one clear definitive solution.

You should seriously look at hiring either temporary staff or an outside consulting firm to maintain your current systems while your staff conducts the inventory.

Your current staff and their supervisors should rotate assignments. That is, the staff should not be permitted to review their own system or hardware and they should be supervised by someone who is not their regular supervisor. This will reduce the chance of a cover-up of a serious problem and still give reassurance that a fresh pair of eyes is inventorying the system and hardware.

You can also use temporary staff members or an outside consulting firm to provide the handful of specialty skills you may need to review some systems and hardware. This is especially true of the technology used with legacy systems.

The Case of...Legacy Systems

A southwest commercial insurance company was facing the task of bringing a vast array of legacy computer systems up to date so the firm did not fall victim to the year 2000 bug. The task facing this firm was monumental.

The firm used 8500 COBOL programs that read and wrote information to 45 IMS databases and six DB2 databases. These programs were the lifeblood of the firm since these were the programs that wrote insurance policies.

The firm spent nine months learning which programs needed to be fixed. What they found was very interesting. The firm could not find the source code for 1500 programs. This meant that if any of these programs needed to be fixed, technicians would first have to decompile the executable program.

Furthermore, to their pleasant surprise, another 1500 programs were not being used by the firm. These were programs that sat on disks and tape taking up space but were never used. Apparently no one on the staff wanted to be responsible for tossing the old programs for fear someone would ask for them again.

Only 2600 programs needed to be fixed. Although this was drastically reduced from the original 8500 programs, the firm was still faced with a monumental task.

In an attempt to ease the demand on mainframe resources during the repair, the firm used Micro Focus Revolve and Express Offloader to copy source code from the mainframe to personal computers. Changes would be made off line where possible using personal computers. The firm then intended to use Mainware's Hourglass 2000 testing tool that works on personal computers. Once the test was completed, the firm planned to use Express Offloader to return the corrected source code to the mainframe for the final testing.

The Assessment Process

Many options are available for assessing the depth of the year 2000 problem at your firm. The one described here is an uncomplicated approach that will work well for a typical organization. You may want to adopt this method for your firm or use this method as a model and modify it to meet your firm's needs.

Let us begin with an understanding of the goal of the assessment process. Once this is known, we can easily design tasks that will let us achieve this objective. The assessment process must identify those systems and hardware that need to be fixed and what steps are necessary to make the repair prior to the first business day of the year 2000.

As mentioned earlier, the assessment process begins with the year 2000 team conducting a careful, painstaking review of the diagrams and documentation produced by the inventory process. This begins with the high-level diagrams of the systems and hardware.

As the team approaches each box on the diagram, they must ask themselves these questions:

- Is this system or hardware affected by the year 2000 bug?
- Is this system or hardware mission critical?

The answers help to group the systems and hardware into manageable groups. The first two groups are

- Systems and hardware not affected; and
- Systems and hardware affected.

Those that are not affected can be removed from consideration. Those that are affected are further broken into two groups:

- Systems and hardware that are mission critical; and
- Those that are not mission critical.

The latter are not removed from consideration but put on a separate list which will be addressed later by the year 2000 team.

Notice that by asking these two questions, the team is able to narrow its focus to systems and hardware that are mission critical. I should point out that while these two questions are easy to ask, they are not necessarily easy to answer. Above all, they do not minimize the effort required by the team to complete the assessment.

Examine the steps necessary to determine if, for example, the payroll system is negatively impacted by the year 2000 bug:

- Each line of each program that comprises the payroll system must be reviewed in detail.

- Databases, tables, and indexes used by these programs must also be reviewed in detail.

- Some database management software such as Sybase could include hidden code called *stored procedures* that are saved with the database—not with the source code of the system.

- The sources of data fed into the system need to be reviewed to determine if they too must be fixed.

- Systems that receive data from the payroll system must also be reviewed to be assured that the restructured date format does not disrupt them.

These are just some of the factors that must be considered by the team when they answer two rather simple questions. Fortunately most of these facts can be ascertained by reviewing the documentation prepared during the inventory process.

The documentation may not directly provide the necessary facts. However, other information such as the technician responsible for the system or hardware or the location of the source code contained in the documentation gives the team a trail to continue their investigation.

The Case of...Programming Standards

A California financial services company is thankful that their systems department strictly enforced standards when developing software applications. These standards, management claims, enable the firm to reduce the inventory process and assessment time in half when dealing with the year 2000 bug.

The firm needed to inventory and assess the impact of the year 2000 bug on about three million lines of code stored in 2500 programs and more than 50 databases. Fortunately, the strict standards of the firm meant that all programs—source code, object code, and executable code—were already accounted for long before the year 2000 bug became a problem.

The firm decided to forgo changing date calculations within the code and instead concentrate on expanding the date file in all the databases. This reduced the unnecessary increase in the size of the program.

Management of the firm projects that complete conversion of all the systems will take 1500 persons-weeks (person week=40 hours over 5 days). This work will be performed by outside vendors.

The Assessment Process and Vendors

Careful attention must be given to software that is acquired from vendors. In the previous chapter, I explored the problems that could arise from licensing and other kinds of agreements involving vendors. It is sufficient to say that legal issues can prevent your firm from making fixes to the software yourself.

Your inventory team assembled sufficient information to indicate whether or not a piece of software or hardware is owned outright by your firm or is entangled with legal requirements from vendors. This information is contained within the documentation prepared by the inventory team.

In a previous section of this chapter, I suggested that your systems and hardware be divided into groups and your year 2000 team focus its attention on systems and hardware that need to be fixed, especially those that are mission critical.

You need to divide these two groups further into:

- Software and hardware your firm owns and can legally fix directly; and

- Software and hardware that are licensed by vendors.

Vendor software includes off-the-shelf software, and hardware includes turnkey systems.

When assessing the situation with vendor software and hardware, your year 2000 team must have your legal staff review contracts, licensing agreements, warranties, and any other documents signed when the software or hardware was acquired.

No assessment of vendor software should proceed unless the results of the legal review are completed. The results will provide the facts necessary to know what kind of action, if any, can be taken by your firm to bring the products into compliance.

In addition to the legal interpretation, your year 2000 team needs to know the penalties assessed if the agreement is breached by your firm. Sometimes these penalties are specified in the agreement and other times they are left for interpretation by both parties or by the courts.

Legal counsel must also advise the team on the impact recent court decisions and settlements of similar cases have on the firm's position. This will give your year 2000 team a reality check as to the likelihood of a successful suit if brought by the vendor and any penalties imposed by the courts.

Legal counsel can also advise whether or not your firm should intentionally breach the contract and fix the software yourself. This option, within practical limitations, is a valid alternative to waiting for the vendor to deliver a year 2000 compliant software package.

Keep in mind that if the vendor fails to deliver the corrected software in a timely fashion, then your mission critical system will fail and possibly jeopardize your business operation. In such a case, the penalty for breach of contract might be less than the penalty experienced when your business is interrupted.

Investigate Vendors Very Carefully

Do not take your software vendors for granted. They too could be experiencing a crisis trying to bring their software into year 2000 compliance. And some vendors may present a calm and controlled demeanor regarding the crises when in reality they are panicking.

There is no way to ensure that your vendor is not bluffing. However, here are a few questions to ask and assessments to make of your software vendors:

- Ask the vendor in writing whether their software is or will be year 2000 compliant by the beginning of 1998. You will need the written statement from the vendor as evidence in case you take legal action. Remember, you will need a year of parallel testing to make sure the fix works. If the vendor promises delivery later than the beginning of 1998, seek other solutions.

- Perform a complete credit check on the vendor and determine the vendor's financial status. You must be comfortable that the vendor has sufficient financial resources to finance the fix.

- Visit the vendor's site and see if there is sufficient technical staff to handle the changes while maintaining the current level of ongoing support.

- Ask the vendor in writing to see the plan and schedule for making the fix.

- Ask your staff who are in day-to-day contact with the vendor's first-line support staff if they have heard of anything changing with the vendor.

Warning Signs

- The vendor refuses to respond in writing. This indicates the vendor is not willing to legally commit to the fix in time. Do not accept any kind of response in place of one in writing.

- The vendor refuses to provide current financial statements certified by an outside auditor. The vendor may be hiding the fact that they are not in a financial position to fix their software.

- The vendor's site shows signs of fiscal problems such as not enough desks, telephones, and computer equipment for the staff.

- The vendor's site shows staffing problems such as more than enough desks, telephones, and computer equipment for the staff. Staff members are the first to realize that the vendor's business is in trouble and they are likely to move to other employment.

- The vendor is not able to show you a plan or schedule for fixing the problem.

• The vendor gradually becomes less responsive to your firm. Calls are not returned and personal contacts are avoided. The staff that normally handles your account no longer does. This could be a sign the vendor is about to go out of business.

The importance of investigating the status of your software and hardware vendor cannot be overemphasized. Your year 2000 team must make an honest assessment of the vendor's capability and desire to make necessary changes to software and hardware to ensure that the software you have will be compliant.

Event Horizon

Your year 2000 team must resist the temptation to rush through the assessment process and make decisions without first exploring the details of each system and piece of hardware. A factor that is easily overlooked during the assessment process is the event horizon for each system.

Some systems process dates beyond the current date. Typically, financial planning software that is used by your firm projects budget, sales, and profits five years ahead of the current date. This is called the system's *event horizon*.

Your year 2000 team must determine the event horizon (how far in the future does the system use dates) for all the systems that must be brought into year 2000 compliance. This is accomplished by examining the kinds of information generated by the system. If the system is used to project anything in the future, chances are good that the system has an extended event horizon (one beyond the year 2000).

Such systems pose a serious concern for the firm, especially if the system is mission critical. The reason is that there are not many years between now and the turn of the century and there is not much time left to fix and fully test the system.

Consider a financial system that projects a firm's financial plans five years forth. In 1997, the system is reporting on what the financial condition of the firm will be in the year 2001. The system is already performing date calculations for the years 2000 and 2001 based on a date that may be inaccurate.

Obviously, the deadline to fix the year 2000 bug in this system passed two years ago. Your year 2000 teams, therefore, must make the assessment of the event horizon one of their top concerns when working through the assessment process.

Here are a few facts that should be ascertained during this assessment process:

- What are the event horizons for all the mission critical systems not in compliance?
- Does the event horizon extend beyond the year 2000?
- What is the impact to the firm when the system performs date calculations today for dates beyond the year 2000?

Answers to these questions can be critical to your firm's operations today! Your system might be producing inaccurate reports which are being used by executives as a basis to make crucial business decisions.

The Case of...The Wrong Information

A northeastern firm specializing in financial planning services for major corporations found themselves in a serious predicament. The firm built a system that received financial and personal information from employees of client firms and projected their retirement benefit.

The firm used their own computers to run the software and clients provided employee data on disks or tapes. The system performed date calculations based on the employee's current age and a reasonable retirement age. The results were used to project the future value of the employee's savings when the employee retired at the prescribed retirement date.

The system then printed all the base financial data along with the assumptions used in the forecast. This information was placed in a personalized report that was sent to the employees of client firms every quarter to coincide with the firm's report of the results of their 401K plan.

Like many companies, this firm knew about the year 2000 bug but thought they had a year before they needed to fix the problem.

This attitude changed when clients began to question the long-term forecast projected by the firm as part of the client's assessment of the year 2000 problem.

Their system worked fine, except the event horizon for the system extended 30 years into the future. Furthermore, the output of the system was one of the products the firm sold to clients. Executives of the firm entered panic mode and began to take steps to correct the problem immediately.

However, until the problem was fixed, the firm reduced charges to clients and printed a notice on every report that information beyond the year 1999 could be questionable. Employees who required accurate information for those years were told to contact the firm by phone and a customer representative would manually calculate the forecast for them.

Triage: Emergency Room Techniques

The assessment process is really your first taste of reality. You learn the exposure that your firm faces and the scope of the project necessary to avoid the year 2000 bug. However, before the year 2000 team can develop a plan to address the problem, the team could find itself in the role of an emergency room physician.

In the previous section, I explored the system's event horizon. This factor determines how soon your team must react to fixing mission critical systems. Systems that are now calculating dates for the year 2000 and beyond are said to be in critical, unstable condition.

This issue for your year 2000 team is to rapidly assess each and every mission critical system to determine if emergency treatment is necessary. Those familiar with emergency medical procedures understand the importance of determining the most critical patient that can be saved. This is called *triage*.

The same technique must be employed when your year 2000 team makes its assessments of mission critical systems that have a long event horizon. The triage process is a method of sorting through—in this case systems and hardware—and determining the priorities of which systems will be "treated." The objective of triage is to maximize the number of systems that are fixed within the shortest time given the limited resources.

Deciding which systems to work on first is difficult since these systems have already been classified as mission critical and all of them are important to the well-being of the firm. Regardless of the challenge of this decision, do not proceed with the planning stage until triage is completed.

Triage calls for systems to be divided into three groups:

1. Systems that will survive without being fixed;

2. Systems that will survive only if the system is fixed; and

3. Systems that will not survive even if the system if fixed.

The first step in the assessment process already placed systems into the first triage group. These are the systems that will not be affected by the year 2000 bug. This means that your year 2000 team must decide if the remaining systems can survive if the fix is performed.

Although the criterion for placing systems into the second group is obvious, your team might have problems deciding which systems fall into the last group; that is, which systems should not be fixed. There is no easy resolution to this problem.

I suggest that the team determine if rebuilding a system is more efficient and less time consuming than fixing the system. If the team determines this is the case, then the system falls into the last category. This category should include systems where:

- You cannot locate the source code;

- A vendor decides not to make the system year 2000 compliant;

- Legal entanglements hinder fixing the problem yourself; and

- You can replace the system with a turnkey system that is already year 2000 compliant.

Simply, a category 3 system is not worth the time and money to fix. This is especially true if you can have a new system built by an outside consulting firm using the latest software tools that will speed development. It's likely that the newer software will offer other advantages. This frees your staff to concentrate on those systems that you know you can fix.

More Triage

Once your systems and hardware are divided into the three triage groups, the triage process must continue. Many firms find the list of fixable systems quite long and in need of prioritization. This too is part of the triage process. Which system should be worked on first? Actually, a few systems can be worked on by different teams at the same time.

The priority of the system is based on the impact it has on the business if it is not year 2000 compliant in time. Each business will have a different criteria for determining the impact a noncompliant system has on the firm's operation. Here are some general questions that should be answered during this process:

- Is the system required to stay government compliant? These are the systems that electronically file reports to government agencies and transfer funds such as those needed to pay payroll taxes.

- Is the system required to maintain basic operations? These are the systems that process orders, maintain payroll, send invoices, and send payments.

- Is the system required to maintain the books and records of the firm? These are the financial systems such as budgeting systems, asset management systems, and financial reporting systems.

I am sure that you can derive more questions like these specific to your industry and firm. The list of these questions should be developed early in the assessment process so the year 2000 team has objective guidelines to follow when performing triage.

Be sure to consider the event horizon of the system when prioritizing your systems for repair. Those systems that have a critical nature to your firm such as those that fall within the guidelines I just mentioned must also be reviewed based on their event horizon.

Those systems that are already miscalculating the date beyond 1999 must be assigned a very high priority since they may already be causing damage to your firm.

Once you have completed the triage you should have a very clear list of systems and hardware that must be fixed in priority order. This list now becomes the basis for your year 2000 team to develop a formal plan to fix these systems.

....

The Plan

Before any work begins on any system or hardware, your year 2000 team must formulate a solid work plan. Two kinds of plans must be built:

- A high-level plan and
- A work plan.

The *high-level plan* lays out the overall strategy for attacking the corporation-wide problem. The *work plan* specifies which staff members must work on what tasks to fix a particular system or hardware.

Let us begin with the high-level plan. The leveling diagram and the triage priority list are used as the basis for the high-level plan. The leveling diagram can be used as a tick and tie list for the year 2000 team to ensure that no system or piece of hardware that should be fixed is overlooked. The priority list is used to determine the order in which a system or piece of hardware must be fixed.

The high-level plan must address the following questions:

- What is the drop-dead deadline for fixing the system?
- What staffing is required to fix the system?
- What facilities and equipment are required by the staff to address the problem?
- What contingencies must be made if the deadline is missed?
- What financial resources are required to support the project?

These are some of the critical factors that must be included in the high-level plan. I am sure that you and your year 2000 team can enhance this list to meet the unique situation of your firm.

The drop-dead deadline is a fixed, unmovable date after which the negative effect of the year 2000 bug interferes with the operation of the firm. Realize that this date is not the deadline for the programmers to make the repair! This is the date when the changes must become a working part of your firm's operation. That is, by the drop-dead deadline technicians have:

- Fully coded the changes;
- Addressed any potential conflicts with other systems; and
- Fully tested the system.

The year 2000 team should establish the drop-dead deadline based solely on the needs of the firm. They should not consider whether or not the fix can be accomplished by the deadline. This might seem unrealistic. You could ask "Why set an unachievable deadline?" The answer is that, achievable or not, your business is in jeopardy the day after the deadline.

Staffing requirements that are necessary to fix the system are determined by the number and kind of tasks that must be performed to correct the problem before the deadline is reached. Your year 2000 team must back into the number of technicians that are necessary and the skills that these technicians must bring to the project.

For this question to be answered, your year 2000 team must explore the details of the system. The team is likely to require the services of experienced project managers who are familiar with the technology used by the system. With their help, the team can make a thorough assessment of the staffing needs.

A common mistake that year 2000 teams make is to set the staffing requirements based on the existing staff. Accept the fact that many firms will require the services of outside technical staff. Let the drop-dead deadline determine the number of new staff members necessary to get the job done on time.

Once the staffing numbers are in place, the year 2000 team is in a position to address the facilities and equipment that are necessary to support the staff as they begin fixing the year 2000 bug.

Here are some of the facilities and equipment that must be considered for the staff:

- Desks, chairs, telephones, and computers;
- Floor space;
- Parking space;

- Support staff such as managers and personnel staff to handle the increased load; and

- General office supplies.

Your present facilities may not be adequate to support the increase in your staff. You may find yourself in search of additional facilities—a process that requires lead time—to be ready for the increased staff. This lead time must be built into the high-level plan.

The Case of....The Tight Squeeze

A financial services firm on the West Coast focused their attention on hiring staff to fix the year 2000 problem. They decided to hire additional staff and temporary staff to address the problem.

Once the assessment was completed, the firm's year 2000 team authorized the immediate hiring of technicians because they realized that other companies would be seeking the same talented individuals.

Problems started to arise almost immediately. No authorization was made for additional support staff. This left the rather limited personnel staff with the task of interviewing and processing an increasingly large number of applications. The applicants included technicians and other persons who were applying for opened positions caused by the normal turnover of staff.

This squeeze backlogged the interview process and caused both the personnel staff and the interviewing managers to work long hours and weekends just to stay on top of the job. Soon, some of the personnel staff themselves were looking for positions outside the firm.

The next problem appeared when the new hires showed up for work. There were not enough desks, telephones, and floor space for them. The problem was left up to low-level managers to resolve. This problem grew beyond the authority of low-level managers to fix.

Many technicians found themselves sitting at old typewriter tables placed up against a post off an aisle. Some technicians accepted the crude accommodations for a reasonable amount of time. However, the firm found that these technicians soon began looking for other employment.

Problems were not over for the firm. There were lines to use the toilet facilities and not enough parking spaces available for the new staff. This led an employee to tip off the building and fire inspectors about the conditions. The inspectors made a surprise visit that resulted in the firm being fined and given less than four weeks to resolve the problem.

This sent the year 2000 team scampering for additional facilities—none of which were in move-in condition. It took three months before the additional facilities were ready for the staff. Furthermore, the firm had to pay a premium to contractors to complete the work.

By the time work was completed, the firm lost 25% of the new technicians they hired and the firm received a negative reputation in the circle of technicians they were trying to recruit. This resulted in the firm paying a premium salary for recruits.

And the problems kept coming. The computer support staff was overwhelmed trying to keep up with the increased demand of the new staff members. Each one needed assistance from computer operations personnel and the technical help desk. Additional staff needed to be hired to support the new technicians.

The year 2000 team lost focus on addressing the year 2000 bug and concentrated on resolving the next problem caused by failure to properly plan for auxiliary services and support staff that were required by an increase in technical employees.

High-Level Contingency Plan

Another critical aspect of the high-level plan is the development of contingencies if the drop-dead deadline cannot be met. The reality is that even with a perfectly executed plan, there is a chance that the object will not be met in time. What happens then?

This question must be answered now, before the emergency occurs, when cool heads are around. This might be the toughest problem for the year 2000 team to address because there probably are no easy solutions.

Here are a few ideas to help your team develop a contingency plan:

- Make arrangements with outside vendors who provide industry-wide computer services to let your firm run its data through their systems (i.e., payroll).

- Contact firms that offer the service of handling orders over their telephones. This might be an alternative to your own order entry system.

- Determine if manual corrections can be made to data and reports until the fixes are completed.

Keep in mind that contingencies might also have an effect on staffing. Someone needs to coordinate activities with vendors. In some cases, temporary systems must be built to handle data feeds with outside vendors. And if you plan any manual intervention, you will need appropriate, trained staff to go into action immediately to keep your business operating.

Another common method used as a backup in case the team fails to meet the deadline is the use of a firm that supplies a contingency site. A problem that is commonly faced by firms who try to fix practically all the systems at the same time is that resources are limited.

This is especially true on mainframe systems where the limited amount of computer resources is divided into production and test regions. Each test region runs all production systems except one system, the system that is being tested. The limited number of test regions restricts the number of tests that can be run at the same time. This bottleneck can dramatically slow down progress and cause frustration among technicians. Since the purchase of additional mainframe resources is not practical, they turn to firms that have equipment available that can be rented on the vendor's site and used for testing.

Furthermore, many corporations have arrangements with firms that provide contingency computer sites. These sites duplicate the computer hardware of the corporation. Technicians require only a few hours to load the corporation's software onto the contingency site's computers before the firm can use the contingency site for testing.

The Work Plan

The final chore of the year 2000 team before the actual work begins to fix the problem is to create a detailed work plan for each system that needs to be brought up to date. A *work plan* is written documentation that lists the milestones of the project. A *milestone* is an event used to indicate progress or lack of progress on the project.

Milestones of a work plan are unique to each system. Here are a few milestones that are commonly found in year 2000 projects. Feel free to add to this list as your needs require.

- Find and locate each program within the system.
- Determine which programs require fixing.
- Determine which databases require fixing.
- Identify codes or routines in each program that must be fixed.
- Correct the database.
- Correct codes or routines in each program.
- Compile the new programs.
- Test the system.
- Complete preproduction requirements.
- Place the system in production.

Notice that some of these milestones have already been reached during the inventory process. This is true, but technicians must confirm the findings of the inventory process then prepare to turn over the code or routine to the technical staff so the repair can be made.

The documentation must also contain clear list of tasks that are necessary to reach a milestone. These tasks are listed beneath the milestone. In the case of the milestone: "Determine which databases require fixing," the year 2000 team must list each database. Furthermore, beneath each database should be listed tables of the databases that need correcting. This is illustrated in Table 4.2.

Determine which databases require fixing

Review the personnel database

    Review the name and address table

    Review the benefits table

    Review the payroll table

    Review the career path table

Table 4. 2 A milestone with related tasks

Next, the year 2000 team needs to assign resources to each task listed on the work plan. A resource is anything that is necessary to complete the task. A programmer is a resource. A region on the mainframe is a resource. A computer terminal is a resource. Collectively these resources can get the job done.

The list of resources that are assigned to the project must be associated with the task in the documentation. This is shown in Table 4.3.

Review the personnel database

Review the name and address table

    Resources: 1 database administrator, 1 terminal, read/write access to the name and address table, 1 copy of the inventory documentation.

Review the benefits table

    Resources: 1 database administrator, 1 terminal, read/write access to the benefits table, 1 copy of the inventory documentation.

Review the payroll table

    Resources: 1 database administrator, 1 terminal, read/write access to the payroll table, 1 copy of the inventory documentation.

Review the career path table

    Resources: 1 database administrator, 1 terminal, read/write access to the career path table, 1 copy of the inventory documentation.

Table 4.3 A milestone with related tasks and related resources needed to complete the task.

The last pieces of information necessary in the work plan are the start and end dates for the milestones and each task. These dates are established by reviewing the priority list created during the assessment process.

The dates used for the work plan must eventually terminate on the day all the systems must be year 2000 compliant. Anyone looking at the overall plan for the year 2000 project must be able to easily move from the high-level plan to any task in any system that needs to be fixed and locate the deadline for the task.

The Work Plan Tool

The next chapter is devoted to tools that help your year 2000 team complete the inventory and assessment processes. There are also tools that will help your staff to properly plan the project. For this purpose, I suggests tools such as Microsoft Project or Project Workbench. There are a number of other project management packages that will work as well, but these are two of the more popular tools.

These tools enable you to insert milestones, tasks, and subtasks into the program, then assign resources and beginning and end dates to each task. With this information, the program projects a termination date for each milestone and for the entire project.

As the plan evolves, you can quickly modify any aspect of the plan such as a missed deadline. The software automatically recalculates beginning and end dates of those tasks that have not been performed.

Furthermore, these tools graphically show you in the form of a Gannt chart the impact a missed deadline has on the entire project. Most of these software packages also create a critical path chart which shows tasks that are dependent on the completion of other tasks. This provides management with sufficient information to reallocate resources during the project in case a task on the critical path begins to fall behind schedule.

Plan the Work, Then Work the Plan

The work plan is probably the most important tool that you have. This plan focuses attention on specific steps that will resolve the potential problem that your company faces in the year 2000.

All the information that is needed to properly manage the project is included in the work plan. Each task is staggered so that more than one task or system can be worked on at the same time, thereby allowing for the most efficient use of resources.

There are beginning and end dates for each task enabling everyone on the project to realize the importance of his or her role in solving the problem. The impact of the missed deadlines is immediately recognized on the work plan long before the effects of the impact are felt on the project.

Steps must be taken to make the work plan an active—if not a central—part of the project. At times some managers put aside the work plan and work more by the seat of the pants rather than using a stable approach to the problem.

The old saying "Plan the Work, Then Work the Plan" has much truth. The work plan is in essence the directions on how to fix the problem. Much time and effort goes into construction of the work plan, so no first-line manager should ignore the work plan to blaze new territory.

The Cost of the Project

I have not mentioned much about assessing the cost of the project. However, fixing the year 2000 problem for your firm can be a very costly experience. The cost estimate can be broken down into soft dollars and hard dollars.

Soft dollars is money that is already in your annual budget. A soft dollar expense is the assignment of a staff programmer to the year 2000 project. The programmer's salary and benefits are already in the budget. The only real loss occurs if the intended assignment is not performed by the programmer.

Hard dollars is money that is above your annual budget. Typically, this is money paid to a consultant who would not have been hired if there was not a year 2000 project. Another hard dollar expense is the additional facilities that are necessary to house an increase in staff. The staff increase too is probably a hard dollar cost.

Basic cost accounting techniques are used to derive a cost for the year 2000 project. You can use the plans and documents talked about in this chapter to form the basis for projected costs. If your firm can use staff personnel to fix the software and stay within the current budget, then the additional cost of the year 2000 project is nil—in hard dollars.

However, once your firm begins spending hard dollars, the cost of the project can escalate rapidly and dramatically. Therefore, your year 2000 team must employ strict budgeting and expense controls before the project is launched.

Another financial aspect that must be seriously considered is the opportunity cost. The money that your firm spends on the year 2000 project above the annual budget is money that could have been earning (or saving) your firm money.

Surplus funds are invested daily by the treasurer of your firm and earn interest. This can be a sizable amount depending on the cash that your firm has available at the close of each business day. The interest revenue is lost if those funds must be diverted to pay the hard dollar expenses of the year 2000 project.

Once surplus funds are depleted, your firm is faced with borrowing cash to pay these new expenses. The cost of borrowing these funds must also be included in the budget for the project. Proper cash flow management and forecasting can keep down the cost of borrowing.

The Case of...The Expenses 00

A major food manufacturer projected the cost of making their software year 2000 compliant by allocating the cost against each line of code that existed in their programs. This method enables the firm's year 2000 team to use this per-line cost to forecast the cost of fixing each program.

The project team estimated they would pay about 50 cents to fix a line of code. This unit cost reflected all the costs that were encountered during the project, not only those expenses that were directly related to changing the line of code.

The assessment process determined that there were 17 million lines of code in all the systems that kept the firm in business.

Of this, 11 million lines needed to be repaired in some fashion. This resulted in a charge of $5.5 million above the current annual budget.

Management of the firm expected that 40 full-time employees would be required to complete the upgrade in time for the turn of the century.

Their analysis revealed that changing the logic of programs that performed date calculations was less costly than expanding the date field in all the databases and adjusting the programs to accept the new size of the date.

Of course, each program needs to be thoroughly analyzed. While changing the logic of the program is the best solution in this case, don't assume that it will work in your situation.

Solutions, Testing, and Implementation

With your inventory completed, assessment made, and a solid plan in place, your year 2000 team must turn over the project to the technical staff to begin to correct the year 2000 problem.

This problem is one that is simple to understand, but thinking that simplistic solutions will resolve the year 2000 bug is naive.

In this chapter I explore the technical side of this problem and show you how to perform the early warning test on your systems. The results of this test verify the conclusion of the year 2000 team and give you a taste of the conditions that will exist at the turn of the century if this project fails.

Once you confirm that the potential year 2000 problem exists in your systems, your attention is directed toward making the fix. Several technical options can be implemented to take care of this problem. You can expand all the current dates to accommodate two more digits. You can build logic into your systems to make assumptions about the current date information. This is called a *sliding date*. You can even perform delicate manipulation of the current date information at the bit level. Called *bit twiddling*, this technique attempts to encode a four-digit date in the space allocated for a two-digit date.

Of course, you can always decide to rebuild your system from scratch and save the headache of locating all the date changes in your systems.

These are just a few of the methods that will be explored in this chapter. At the end of the chapter, you will see how those changes must be tested and the implications that are involved in placing the changed systems into operation before the clock strikes 12 on December 31, 1999.

The Early Warning Test

What will really happen to your systems at the turn of the century? Throughout this book I have speculated on the dangers that could lurk on New Year's Eve in the year 1999. You can end this speculation and look ahead and see for yourself the impact this problem can have on your systems.

Give your systems the early warning test. This is a rather benign operation for most systems. The test involves resetting the system clock on your computer, then let your computer react naturally as if the year 2000 has arrived. A word of caution: Be sure that the change of date does not interfere with the current operation of your systems. This technique may not be used on systems other than personal computers. Some systems require that the system administrator reset the date and other systems require that the entire system be replicated onto separate equipment so not to interfere with normal operations.

Try these steps on your personal computer:

- Disconnect your personal computer from your local-area network. This is to prevent your personal computer from using the date setting on the network in place of the internal date on your computer.

- Back up all the systems stored on your personal computer. You can always restore your systems from this backup copy in case the early warning test has a negative impact on the operation of your computer or systems.

- Set your system's clock to 23:55. This is five minutes before midnight.
- Set the date on your system to December 31, 1999.
- Turn off your computer for about five minutes.
- Turn on your computer.
- Check the date on your computer. This should be January 1, 2000.

All the systems running on your personal computer should react as if the year 2000 bug has struck. If your computer system's clock does not show the correct date, then you know that you must upgrade your hardware because all the systems running on the computer will be using an inaccurate date.

Many computers will show the wrong century. Others will show an incorrect date altogether. There have been reports that some systems will move into the twenty-first century, but skip the year 2000 and go directly to 2001. A few could crash because the system clock reported a wrong date.

However, if the date is correct, you can continue with the early warning test. Run all the systems that normally run on the computer and watch them carefully. Print all reports and check the data carefully to determine if the report is affected by the problem.

Completely test all the systems that run on the computer. Make various inquiries into the database to see if you receive the results that you expect. Be sure the data sorts properly. The year 2000 bug can have a dramatic effect on indexes and sorting procedures.

If all goes well, then your personal computer systems are probably not affected by the year 2000 bug. However, chances are that some if not all of your systems that use dates will have some problems.

Networked Systems

Systems that are shared on a server require a similar but different kind of early warning test. Follow the same procedure that I recommend for testing your personal computer. However, instead of resetting the system's date on your personal computer, reset the network's system's date on the server.

Be sure that you have taken the necessary precautions to back up the complete server before running this test. Failure to do so could be catastrophic. The date change could invalidate software licenses which means the software that you counted on will no longer work. The software thinks that the time is right to pay more money to the vendor to renew your software license—even if you do not owe anything.

Another serious problem that could occur is that all passwords including that of the system administrator expire because the network date is beyond the expiration date. This could result in the need to reinstall the networking operating system.

A similar test can be performed on workstations. A system administrator can reset the system date to reflect the change in the century. The same precautions apply when testing workstation applications. Back up your system but do not disconnect the workstation.

The early warning test for mainframe applications is also performed by resetting the system's date. Your operations staff needs to create a test region that mirrors your complete production environment. The system's date is only changed in this test region.

Regardless of the platform, the results of the early warning test are only as good as the data that you use for the test. I strongly recommend that you use a typical day's production data as input data for the test. You can then compare processed data produced by the acid test against processed data produced during a typical day's production—same day and same data. The results of this comparison gives you a good idea of what the first business day will be like in the next century.

··

Reported Test Results

The press has reported about how specific software and hardware will be affected by the year 2000 bug. I will review some of these reports here so that you will have a feeling for where potential problems lie.

However, do not assume that you will have the same experience as those reported in the press. You must still validate whether or not these reports are correct for your software and hardware. Always retest before making a decision based on published reports.

A problem is reported with the time command in TSO when the date is 01/01/2000. This command returns the date as January 1, 1900. COBOL/370 applications running in TSO, however, are able to process dates in the next century correctly.

Some personal computer products have also been reported to have difficulty with the new century. These include AST computers that have R1.02 GA-486US bios; Micro-Pro with the award modular bios version 3.2-00nm; COMPAQ: Proliant 4100; Hewlett Packard Vectra M2 486/66; and DeskPro 575.

Contact the manufacturers of these products to determine if and when an upgrade will be available. If no upgrade is forthcoming within a reasonable time, then consider replacing the equipment.

On the positive side, published reports state that the Gateway 2000 P5-90; DEC Venturis 4100; and the Macintosh PowerBook can handle dates into the next century.

Although Windows 95 passes the year 2000 test, this product does have a date problem. Reports state that Windows 95 has a date range from 1980 through 2099. Once again, are developers creating applications with a built-in destruction date? I guess Microsoft assumes by the time 2100 comes around there will be new software and any problems with the dates will be someone else's problem. Remember, though, that similar assumptions got us into this problem!

Windows 95 is ready for the next century, but some of your old Windows 3.1 programs may be falling behind. There have been reports that

Paradox for Windows is convinced that the 00 represents 1900. Then there is Version 3 of Quicken running on MS-DOS 6 that interprets 01/01/2000 as 1/1/1901—not even 1900. And reportedly when the date is set at 12/31/1999, the next day becomes 01/04/1980. Again, these are just examples.

Mainframe applications that use ADA such as those used by defense contractors and government agencies could be in for trouble. A problem has been reported in the day-of-week calculation. ADA handles the transition from one century to the other and the leap year without any problems. However, the day of week is off by a day at least from March 1, 2000, through February 28, 2001.

As mentioned earlier, these are some of the problems reported in the press. You still must confirm these findings for your computer before deciding to complain to the vendors.

Expand Two-Digit Years to Four Digits

The early warning test gives you a quick answer to the question "How will my systems perform on the first business day of the next century?" Now let us turn our attention to fixing the problem. Of course, this test does not tell you if data sent to your system by another firm is year 2000 compliant. You need to examine that incoming file to determine if the dates are in compliance.

Several options are available to correct the year 2000 bug. One of these is the most obvious. That is, insert the century digits—the 19 and 20—everywhere a date is stored or calculated. This solution for some applications is rather straightforward and requires only a few hours work once all the date locations are found.

For other applications, however, inserting the century digits is a very time-consuming and complex task and requires you to seriously consider other options before adding two characters to every date.

There are generally two areas in a typical system where you can insert the century digits into a date: a date calculation within the program and in a database where the date data is stored. These are practically the only sources of dates in most systems.

Date calculations fall into several categories. The most common involve calculations that:

- Use a date retrieved from a field in a database (i.e., employment date);

- Use the system's date (i.e., today's date);

- Encode the date into another field (i.e., serial number 97-12345);

- Display all or a portion of the date in a report (i.e., day of the order);

- Determine the lapse of time (i.e., days a bill is overdue); and

- Use dates in a function (i.e., determining the day of week).

These are the more common ways in which a calculation in a program uses a date. Each one of these calculations creates a different problem when attempting to correct the missing two-digits from the year.

Calculations: Date Retrieved from a Field in a Database

Certain assumptions are made when a program reads a date field from a database or from a table. The first assumption is that the information contained in the field is a date. The second assumption is the format of the date. Both assumptions are valid because the programmer writes routines based on known data types and formats contained in the database.

However, these assumptions could become invalid depending on the method used to fix the year 2000 bug. The format of the date field could change from mm/dd/yy to mm/dd/yyyy to include the two additional digits to represent the century.

Adjustments may need to be made to routines that read the date from the database if the date is compared with a date in a different format. A situation could arise where a date contained in data received from another firm is compared to a date in your firm's database. This commonly occurs in programs that electronically perform bank reconciliation. Your firm might have modified the date format in your database; however, the other firm might not have.

You can fix this problem by first assuming years earlier than 50 are in the twenty-first century, then modifying the date comparison routine within your program. A method of doing this is shown in Listing 5.1. An assumption is made in this example: Dates are date types not strings (text) and therefore must be converted to a string (text) so that modification of the date can be made.

This listing is written in pseudocode. Once you understand the logic of the routine, you can translate the code into the appropriate language for your system. You will also notice that the pseudocode contains several functions (procedures) that are commonly found in most language libraries. These are date-to-string conversion functions, the substring function, and the string-to-number function.

In Listing 5.1, the problem is that other_date, which is the date received from an outside source, does not use the century digits. Your database has been changed to use a four-digit year. A comparison of the two dates may not match depending on the language used to make the comparison.

You can circumvent this problem by first converting both dates to string data types. Next, insert the century digits into the other_date before the dates are compared. This is possible by using a substring function that breaks apart the other_date into components. Years earlier than 50 are assumed to be in the twenty-first century.

In Listing 5.1, the yy portion of the date is separated from the mm/dd/ segment of the date. Each piece is assigned to variables. The yy component is then temporarily changed from a string (text) to a number value, which is compared in an if statement expression. If this value is less than 50, then the routine assumes that the two century digits should be 20, otherwise these digits are 19.

Based on the results of this comparison, the routine assembles the necessary pieces of the date to form a new date, which is assigned to the new_date variable. Now both dates are in the correct date format allowing a comparison to be made.

Listing 5.1 *Date matching routine fix.*

```
other_date = ConvertDateToString(mm/dd/yy)

your_date = ConvertDateToString(mm/dd/yyyy)

tmp_date1 = substring(other_date, 1, 6)
tmp_date2 = substring(other_date,7,2)
```

```
if (MakeNumber(tmp_date2) < 50)
   new_date = tmp_date1 + "20" + tmp_date2
else
   new_date = tmp_date1 + "19" + tmp_date2
end if
if (new_date = your_date)
   print "Match"
else
   print "No Match"
end if
```

Another common problem that is encountered is that the date field in the database is not increased to accommodate the century digits in the year. Your program, however, must use the corrected date value in calculations. Listing 5.2 illustrates a technique that can be written into the program to resolve this issue each time the program runs. This routine does not correct the problem with the date field, but provides a workaround that allows your program to make the necessary corrections before using the date value.

This routine begins with a comment line (#) indicating that the field in the database is called dField and contains a date in the format mm/dd/yy. For one of many reasons (which I discuss later in this chapter), the format of this field cannot be changed to mm/dd/yyyy. So, you need to write code that converts the date to the four-digit year format.

The initial task is for this routine to read the value of the field into the variable date_field, which is then converted to a string (text) and assigned to the variable old_date. This value is then stripped into two components using the substring function as is illustrated in Listing 5.1.

The routine determines the correct century digits using the MakeNumber function, then reconstructs the date into the new format and assigns the new value to the variable temp_date3. The assumption is made that years earlier than 50 are in the twenty-first century. This variable is converted from a string (text) to a date using a function and is assigned to the new_date variable.

The final step is to change lines of code within the program to use the new_date variable in place of the dField value from the database. There are various tools that can be used to find all the places where the dField value is used in a system. I will review these tools in the next chapter.

Listing 5.2 *The size of the data field in the database is not increased.*

```
#The date format in the dField field in the database
is mm/dd/yy.
read dField into date_field
old_date = ConvertDateToString(date_field)
tmp_date1 = substring(old_date, 1, 6)
tmp_date2 = substring(old_date,7,2)
if (MakeNumber(tmp_date2) < 50)
  tmp_date3 = tmp+date1 + "20" + tmp_date2
else
  tmp_date3 = tmp+date1 + "19" + tmp_date2
end if
new_date = Convert StringToDate(tmp_date3)
```

Some database management software may not accept the yyyy date format. As shown in Listing 5.2, you can easily write a routine that converts the old date format (i.e., yy) to the new date format (i.e, yyyy) before using the value in a calculation.

However, a few firms may force a database solution. This means that the four-digit year must be stored on the database even if the database management software does not accept this format.

One method to do this is to add a character field to the database, then populate this new field with a restructured date value. This results in two, same date values stored for each record in the database. One date value is in a date field in the current date format (mm/dd/yy) and the other is in a character type field in the four-digit year date format (mm/dd/yyyy).

However, this solution can cause a serious ripple effect that will be discussed later in this chapter. For now, however, I address two more immediate problems. The first of which is how to populate the new field with the restructured date format. Listing 5.3 shows how this is done.

The routine consists of a loop that steps through each record in the databases and continues until the end-of-file marker is reached. For each pass, the routine reads the value of dField that contains the two-digit year date value in the database and assigns the value to the date_field variable. The assumption is made that years earlier than 50 are in the twenty-first century.

The date_field is then converted to a string value which is dissected by the substring function as discussed previously in this section. The date is then restructured and saved in the new character type field called cField in the database. The routine then moves onto the next record in the database and repeats the same procedure.

Once all the restructured date values are stored in the database, programs that use the old date format value must be modified. Listing 5.4 shows a single line that handles this issue. Routines that read dField from the database must be changed to read sField.

Furthermore, the value of sField must be converted to a string before the value can be used with existing date calculations. In Listing 5.4, I suggest reading data from the database once, converting the value to a date data type, then assigning the value to a variable. The variable name can then be used wherever reference is made to dField in the program.

Listing 5.3 *Populate a character field with a restructured date value.*

```
#dField in database is in mm/dd/yy format. cField is
a character field.
do while (not end of file)
  read dField into date_field
  date_field = ConvertDateToString(date_field)
  tmp_date1 = substring(date_string, 1, 6)
  tmp_date2 = substring(date_string,7,2)
  if (MakeNumber(tmp_date2) < 50)
    new_date = tmp_date1 + "20" + tmp_date2
  else
```

```
      new_date = tmp_date1 + "19" + tmp_date2
   end if
   replace cField with new_date
end do
```

Listing 5.4 *Using the date value from a character data type field of a database.*

```
date_field = ConvertStringToDate(sField)
```

Calculations: Encoding a Date into Another Field

A common date calculation is to use a portion of the current date as a segment of a number such as is the case with a serial number. A serial number typically consist of an incremented number, a static number, and either all or a portion of the current date. Collectively these components are assembled and used as an identifier for a record in a database.

The date component of a serial number is typically in a fixed format that is difficult to change. This serial number illustrates this point: 019854010004. This number has four components: month, year, product, and unit. The month is 01 and the year is 98. The product number is 5401 and the unit number is 0004.

Each component of a serial number is created using a unique method. The month and year are identified from the computer system's date. The product number is usually hard coded into the program or read from a field in a database. The latter method provides greater flexibility; however, either method is used in production systems. The unit number is read from a field in the database. After the unit number is read from the database, the program increments the number and places the new number back into the field.

The problem that occurs with the turn of the century occurs in the routine that extracts the month and year from the system's date. Assume that the system's date is in the format mm/dd/yy. Listing 5.5 illustrates the routine that can be used to extract that month and year from the current date, which is a fairly straightforward process. The SystemDate is converted to a string (text), and is then assigned to the cur_date variable. The components are then extracted, restructured, and assigned to the comp1 variable to form component 1 of the serial number.

Listing 5.5 *Extracting the month and year from the system's date.*

```
cur_date = ConvertDateToString(SystemDate)
sMonth = substring(cur_date,1,2)
sYear = substring(cur_date,7,2)
comp1 = sMonth+sYear
```

However, if the system's date is changed to include the century digits, then this portion of the serial number routine will come up with the wrong year. All the years will be either 19 or 20 depending on whether the new century has arrived. This is because the system's date will be mm/dd/yyyy with the first two-digits being either 19 or 20. The routine in Listing 5.5 merely extracts the first two characters of the year, assuming these characters represent the year not the century.

Dates and Serial Numbers

A solution to incorporating the date as part of the serial number is to change the way the serial number is created; that is, modify the year component to use all four-digits of the year. While this is technically possible, a ripple effect must be considered.

This begins with the size of the field that contains the serial number.

- Has this field been increased to accept two new characters?
- Will the other serial numbers have to be modified and the year component changed to four-digits?
- If existing serial numbers are not changed, how will the system handle both serial number formats, especially if serial numbers are sorted by year?
- Is there room for these two-digits on the product or wherever the serial number is printed? Some design aspects of the product may have to be reconsidered to accommodate a larger serial number.

These are just a few of the subsequent problems that can occur when the date component of the serial number is changed. You can probably identify other problems like these that are unique to your business or industry.

Maintaining a Serial Number's Integrity

An alternative to the preceding approach is to modify the program to extract just the year component of the date. This is shown in Listing 5.6, which is nearly identical to the code in Listing 5.5 except the substring function is told to read the correct character position of the year.

If the year is 01/01/1997, then the substring function reads characters 9 and 10 to identify the year component of the date. In the previous listing, if the date is 01/01/97, the substring function reads characters 7 and 8 to capture the two-year digits.

This method maintains the integrity of the existing serial numbers and ensures that new serial numbers blend appropriately with the current system and database. Of course, there is an inherent problem with this method. If the product remains in production for 100 years, then there could be confusion over the year component of the serial number. Is 99 2099 or 1999? The answer should be obvious for most products. Very few products remain the same for a hundred years.

Listing 5.6 *Extracting the month and year from the system's date when the system's date has changed to mm/dd/yyyy.*

```
cur_date = ConvertDateToString(SystemDate)
sMonth = substring(cur_date,1,2)
sYear = substring(cur_date,9,2)
comp1 = sMonth+sYear
```

Calculations: Display All or a Portion Of a Date in a Report

Information in a database or information received directly from an outside source is typically presented to the user of the system as a report. A report can be displayed on the screen or printed on paper. Reports are traditionally identified by name and by date.

In reports, the date can represent the date the report is created and also dates of the information contained in the report. There can be many kinds of dates on the report including date information used as data in the report or as titles for either columns or for the report itself. Technicians must review each date that is used on the report to determine if the source of the date is year 2000 compliant.

There is very little that can be done if the date on the report is read directly from the computer's system date. If the system's date is not year 2000 compliant, then neither is the date on the report. The only solution available is to change the report so that the system's date is not directly used on the report. Instead, the date can be restructured from the system's date to include the century digits using routines discussed previously in this chapter.

Of course, this is dependent on how the report is created. A report that is created using report-generating software may not enable a programmer to modify the date directly. However, a report that is produced directly from source code can be modified.

Many report-generating software packages enable the programmer to specify a date format by using a drop-down list box or a regular list box. In either case, all the available date formats are contained on the list and can be selected with a click of the mouse button.

Nearly all of these tools provide a date format that is year 2000 compliant. That is, a programmer is able to find a date format on the list in the format mm/dd/yyyy. Therefore, a date displayed on a report can be reformatted to represent the century digits in the year.

Two factors must be considered when making such an adjustment in your report. First, date information and other information on the report might have to be repositioned on the report to allow for the new two-digits. This is also true if report-generating software is used to create the report.

The other factor is the date itself. Changing the format of a date on the report does not solve the year 2000 compliant problem. The source of the date data determines whether the century is 19 or 20. The format of the date only determines if the century digits are to be displayed.

How do you correct the problem if the source of the date is not year 2000 compliant and report-generating software is used to create the report? Since you probably cannot add code to the report-generating software to restructure the date on the report, you must look elsewhere to restructure the date.

I recommend that you consider adding another field to the database. I talk more about this technique later in this chapter. For now, all you need to know is the solution methodology. The new field need only hold 10 characters. Write a routine that reads the noncompliant date in each record, restructure the date to add the appropriate century, then save the restructured date into the new field.

This routine, shown previously in this chapter, must be included in all programs that store a date in the database. This ensures that all new records contain the appropriate century digits. You can also run this routine as a utility program to convert existing date data to include the century.

Once the conversion process is completed, you must modify the report to use the new date field in the database rather than the old date field. The report then becomes year 2000 compliant, assuming that the date format on the report is changed to display the century digits.

A word of caution: Text used as column headings on reports created by report-generating software can contain the last two-digits of the year (e.g., sales 97). This text could be the name of the field in the database and not text generated by the report-generating software.

There are two ways to modify the column heading to include the century digits: modify the field name or replace the field name with text produced by the report-generating software. The easiest and possibly the only solution is to enter new text for the column heading directly into the report-generating software. Some database management software makes changing an existing field name difficult to perform.

Calculations: Determine the Lapse of Time

Calculations of the lapse of time in months, days, and years are frequently performed by systems that are affected by the year 2000 bug. The lapse of time is calculated using two methods: using the addition or subtraction arithmetic operator or by calling a function.

Some computer languages can perform date calculations on date values such as deriving 1 year by subtracting 01/01/98 minus 01/01/97. Of course, the year 2000 bug causes this logic to return a false result when the computer is told to subtract 01/01/00 minus 01/01/99.

A way to correct this problem is by adjusting the dates prior to performing the calculation. Listing 5.7 contains a routine that fixes this problem. The assumption is made that years earlier than 50 are in the twenty-first century.

In this routine, two date fields are read from a database. Each of these dates is converted to a string, then broken into components, and modified with the appropriate century digits. The modified version of these dates is converted back to the date data type before the lapsed time calculation is performed.

Listing 5.7 Correcting dates before calculating lapsed time.

```
read dField1 into date_field1
read dField2 into date_field2
sfield1 = ConvertDateToString(date_field1)
sfield2 = ConvertDateToString(date_field2)
tmp_date1 = substring(sfield1, 1, 6)
tmp_date2 = substring(sfield1,7,2)
if (MakeNumber(tmp_date2) < 50)
new_date1 = tmp_date1 + "20" + tmp_date2
else
    new_date1 = tmp_date1 + "19" + tmp_date2
end if
tmp_date1 = substring(sfield2, 1, 6)
tmp_date2 = substring(sfield2,7,2)
```

```
if (MakeNumber(tmp_date2) < 50)
new_date2 = tmp_date1 + "20" + tmp_date2
else
   new_date2 = tmp_date1 + "19" + tmp_date2
end if
date_field1 = ConvertStringToDate(new_date1)
date_field2 = ConvertStringToDate(new_date2)
lapse_time = date_field2 - date_field1
```

A different approach must be used if a function is called to perform the lapsed time calculation. Although each function is unique, most of them have a similar characteristic in that two dates are required to be passed to the function and the function returns the lapsed time.

In the next section, you will encounter the problems that can occur if a function is not year 2000 compliant and the steps to follow to deal with this situation. The same resolution applies to functions that perform lapsed time calculation.

Calculations: Use Dates in a Function

Pieces of programs commonly called *functions* may require the program to pass date information to the function so that the function can properly perform a calculation. The function could determine the interval between dates or determine a value such as the future value of an investment. The result of the calculation is then returned by the function to your program.

Several problems can arise from the use of functions within your program. One problem is the date format that is accepted by the function. This format cannot be changed unless the function is created by your firm. Typically, this is not the case. Instead, functions are purchased as part of the programming language or are purchased from a third party.

This poses a serious problem when attempting to fix the year 2000 problem. Regardless of where date formats are changed throughout your program, the program may still need to provide the function with the old date format, which may not be year 2000 compliant.

Another problem that can occur when functions used by your program are not year 2000 compliant is that if you do not have access to the source code for the function nor the right to change the code within the function, then you must rely on a third party to repair the function. Of course, there is no guarantee that the new function will be delivered on time.

Until the new function arrives, you must modify your program to reconstruct the year 2000 date value to match the requirements of the old function. You can modify the routines described previously in this chapter to perform the date restructuring. However, this is only half of the problem. While you provide the function with the required information, you must determine if the results of the function remain valid.

If the return value of the function is correct, then you have temporarily resolved the year 2000 compliant problem until the new function arrives. Otherwise, you must consider reverse engineering the function, then build a new function.

Reverse engineering requires that your firm follow specific procedures to make sure that you have not violated any rights of the third party who supplied you with the original function. There are two steps in the reverse engineering process. First, a technician who is not familiar with your application nor the function must review the input and output of the function and develop functional specifications for the function. Functional specifics describe in English how the function receives data, performs the calculation, and returns the results to the program.

Next, the functional specifications must then be turned over to another technician. This technician, too, must have no knowledge whatsoever of the function supplied by the third party. The technician must build a new function based solely on the functional specifications developed by the other technician.

This method provides a clean break between the function purchased by your firm and the function created internally which is year 2000 compliant. Any questions about this procedures should be discussed with your attorney to ensure that the third-party vendor does not have any claim against your firm for violating their rights.

....

Expanding Date Fields and Changing Data: A Potentially Happy Alternative

So far in this chapter you have explored ways to change parts of your programs so that your programs become year 2000 compliant. Changing your program is just one of the ways that you can bring your systems into the twenty-first century. The other method is to change the date data in the databases read by your systems.

Date fields in your databases are probably in the form of mm/dd/yy. You can make these fields year 2000 compliant by expanding each date field to accept the century digits. Once this is accomplished, you may not need to modify your programs or your reports.

Before you rush to modify your database, you must consider the negative impact that field expansion can have on your operation. The obvious drawback of increasing the size of the date field is that the size of the data file itself grows in size.

I briefly explored this previously in this book, but the seriousness of this factor requires that I mention this once more. Make two assumptions: There are five date fields in a database and the database contains 1 million records. Modifying these date fields could require 10 million more bytes of space if each additional digit is stored as a byte.

Besides requiring additional space on a disk, tape, or CD, you have also increased the time necessary to transfer the entire database such as when you make a backup copy of the data.

And there could be a ripple effect. Assume that overnight data processing begins by archiving the current database. The expanded fields in our case require movement of 10 million more bytes before the remaining overnight processing jobs are run.

The additional data transfer could cause the remaining jobs to be delayed and might impact the successful completion of other jobs. Systems may not be ready in time for the next day's business. If this is your solution, you may need to adapt to the added date in your database in a manner that is workable.

The Case of ...The Tardy Production Schedule

A Texas financial institution modified three large databases to bring their systems in compliance with the year 2000. These databases contained the books and records of the firm, employee information, and an order processing system. Each database contained at least a dozen places where technicians felt that the date field needed to be expanded to include the century digits.

The firm launched the Year 2000 project after spending four months studying the potential negative effect that the year 2000 bug would have on each of the company's systems. They laid out detailed plans on how to approach the problem. These plans included staffing requirements and other factors that entered into correcting the problem.

Even with all of this planning, a serious problem arose when the firm placed the changes into production. Many of the overnight production systems failed to work properly, especially those that sent and received data to and from other systems. Every program seemed to be out of sync with the other systems.

This was puzzling since changes to the current system were relatively minor and were fully tested. Prior to these changes being made, all the production systems ran smoothly.

At the heart of the problem was the expansion of 36 date fields in the three databases. It seemed that the additional time required to process these bytes of information extended the overnight batch production schedule.

Jobs started automatically according to a particular time in the schedule. The assumption was made that jobs earlier in the schedule ran on time. Some of those jobs processed data while others transmitted or received data systems within and outside the firm.

Some jobs took longer to process the data because of the additional bytes in the date fields. Other jobs worked fined but required earlier jobs to have completed processing, which was not the case. The time frame to send to and receive data from outside systems came and went without any transmission because other jobs were not finished processing.

After nearly a week of experiencing this problem, the technical staff adjusted the schedule to accommodate the extended processing time. This adjustment was made with great reservations since no more time slots were available in the overnight product cycle. Any future extension of the schedule will cause some batch jobs to run during the first few hours of the business day.

The Invisible Problem

Modification of the date fields can also impact areas of operation that are not visible to the end user or to programmers. Date fields might be used as keys to index files. An *index file* helps you find information quickly in a large database by looking up one field or a combination of fields. This field(s) exists both in the index file and in the database. Along with this field(s) in the index file, there is a reference to the complete record in the database.

The problem occurs when the date field in the database that is used as a key to an index is expanded in the database only. Assuming that the values in this database field are changed to include the century digits, then the index and the date field no longer match.

When you ask the system to search by date for a particular record in the database, the system will report that no such record exists. The system looks in the index file first where the date is specified as mm/dd/yy. However, the date in the database is mm/dd/yyyy as is the search criteria.

The only solution is for you to rebuild all the indexes that are associated with the database. Keep in mind that the size of the index file will probably increase, adding to the requirements for resource space (i.e., disk) and transfer time during the archiving process.

Another factor of expanding the size of a date file is the impact this has on sorting records in the database. Your system may sort records using the date field. Say that dates are stored as mm/dd/yy. In fact, there are a million records that have five date values in this format. You decide to increase the size of these fields to accommodate two century digits. This results in the date fields being able to handle either mm/dd/yy or mm/dd/yyyy formats.

A problem can occur if only new date values are in the mm/dd/yyyy format and the existing date data is in the mm/dd/yy format. Insert actual dates into these patterns and see what happens when your system sorts the database by these dates.

An existing date value is 01/01/99 and a new date value might be 01/01/1998 (assume these dates have nothing to do with the current date). Records associated with the year 1998 come after records with the year 99 when the system sorts records by these dates. The number 99 is less than the number 1998.

You can avoid this problem by inserting the century digits in all date fields using a routine similar to those I illustrated earlier in this chapter.

Some Common Sense When Expanding Date Fields

The expansion of a date field can have serious repercussions on the operation of your system as I pointed out in the previous section. Therefore, you should not rush to use this method to solve the year 2000 problem. Instead, sit back and use a little common sense.

Ask yourself if the date is impacted by the year 2000 bug. By this I mean will the date, as is, continue to work successfully in your system? If so, then there is no need to increase the size of the corresponding date field. Not all dates have to be changed to include the two century digits.

Generally speaking, if the date is not used as a key to an index, part of a sort, or in a date calculation, and will not be confused with other dates, than there probably is no reason to insert the century digits. Not doing so can save resources and minimize the impact of making the database year 2000 compliant.

Even if the date is used for sorting records in the database, you may not need to modify the format of the date. Some sort routines are used to group like records and not necessarily place records in sequential order by date.

All that is necessary is for all the records for the same year to be grouped together. In such a case, there is no need to insert the century digits in the date since this will not affect the operation of the sort routine.

Consider the database that has five date fields and a million records. As I pointed out earlier in this chapter, the insertion of the century digits adds 10 million bytes to the size of the database. However, assume that only one date field is used as the key to an index. None of the other date fields needs to be expanded. The database need only increase by 2 million bytes, and other associated files with the database such as the copy book (mainframe applications) also do not have to change.

Other factors also come into play when fields are expanded. The database must be off line when these changes are made. In many database systems, modification of the size of a field requires that a new database be created and all the data copied from the old to the new database. You must determine if the old database can remain off line while this process is completed. Furthermore, every aspect of the system must be thoroughly tested before the database—and the system—is brought back on line.

Another common problem with some nonrelational databases is that there is no room to expand the record size. You cannot add the two century digits to any date field. In this case, you must consider changing routines in your program to make the date data year 2000 compliant where necessary.

Even if you are able to insert the century digits, you must review all the programs in your system to determine if routines that handle dates are capable of working with a four-digit year compared with the existing two-digit year. If not, then you must modify the code as well as modify date fields in the database.

Date fields in a relational database can always be increased, even if a new table of the database must be created. A word of caution: A relational database can contain many tables. Each table contains records. Records in two tables are linked by a common field. If the date field is used as the common field, then you must expand both fields. Expanding just one field will make each field unique and prevent the two tables from being linked.

Another factor that must be addressed is the search criteria that are used by ad hoc reporting tools. These are tools that allow users of the system to pick field names from a list to create their own search criteria and reports. You must review how these tools will work with the new date format.

Sliding Dates

Logic can be built into your programs to interpret the current two-digit year as being in either the twentieth or twenty-first century depending on the current year. This technique is called *sliding dates* or *windowing*.

Your system determines the century of a date based on a 100-year window. On New Year's the 100-year window slides forward one year. Say that the 100-year window begins with 01/01/60 and extends through to December 31, 2059. Very simple logic can be added to your program to determine the century. Listing 5.8 illustrates this logic.

Listing 5.8 Creating a sliding 100-year window.

```
#This year is stored in a database and is used to set
the beginning range for the
#100-year window.
read begin_yr into from_yr
cur_date = Convert DateToString(05/04/97)
temp1 = substring(cur_date,1,6)
temp2 = substring(cur-date,7,2)
temp_yr = ConvertStringToNumber(temp2)
if (temp_yr >=from_yr)
new_date1 = temp1 + "19" + temp2
else
new_date1 = temp1 + "20" + temp2
end if
```

The routine in Listing 5.8 first reads the beginning year of the 100-year window, which in this case is 60. Next, the current date is converted to a string and broken down into two components, one of which is the year. The year is then converted into a number that is compared to the beginning year of the 100-year window. If the current year is greater than or equal to the beginning year, then the current century is assumed to be the twentieth century. Otherwise, the century is assumed to be the twenty-first century.

At the beginning of each new year, the value of the beginning year in the database must be incremented, thereby sliding the window to the next 100-year range. Although the range of the window is modified, the routine as shown in Listing 5.8 does not change.

This technique seems to resolve the year 2000 compliant problem for many systems. Creating a sliding window does not require any expansion of date fields in the database. Furthermore, programs need only be changed once to accommodate this date calculation.

However, there are drawbacks to using this technique that may not make this an acceptable solution for all applications. An obvious problem occurs with applications that have data spanning 100 years such as some life insurance systems.

In addition, this solution does not resolve problems that occur when dates are used as keys to index files or sort routines. In both cases, the century digits must be inserted into the date for these to work properly. The sliding window does not insert the two century digits.

Bit Twiddling

Some firms push the limits of technology to resolve the year 2000 compliant problem by manipulating the physical positioning of bits that are used to represent the two-digit year. This entails a low-level fix to the problem that requires a very high precision, otherwise even the current date can become corrupted.

Typically dates are represented as numbers. Numbers are represented as a setting of bits. A *bit* is a binary digit which is either a 0 or 1 and a set of 8 or 16 bits is used to represent the value of a number.

Clever technicians are capable of resetting these bits to represent a four-digit year instead of the current two-digit year. In nontechnical terms, the technician stuffs four-digits into the physical positions of two digits.

The advantage of this technique is that there is little disruption to the data flow and no additional space is required for the century digits. No additional bits are added to the data.

The disadvantage is that making this change requires a high degree of precision by a technician that may not be available on your staff.

Bridge Program

A bridge program is a lifesaver for many firms when the deadline grows near and the pile of changes is still a mile high. A *bridge program* converts a record layout to another record layout and is used as a way of interfacing a year 2000 compliant program with a program that is not in compliance. A bridge program provides the flexibility that is required by applications that need to communicate with other systems, many of which are not under the control of the company.

The logic of a bridge program is uncomplicated. The program reads a record from a compliant database then reformats each date field to meet the requirement of the noncompliant database. The modified record is then saved to the noncompliant database.

The same logic can be incorporated into routines that transmit data across a network to a remote computer. That is, the conversion of the date data is performed on the fly. Listing 5.9 shows the logic that is in a typical bridge program.

This bridge program bridges a noncompliant database (database1) with a compliant database (database2) and makes the assumption that years earlier than 50 are in the twenty-first century. First, the program reads a record from the noncompliant database. There are only three fields in this database: date, first name, and last name. Each of these values is read into a variable.

Listing 5.9 *Creating a bridge program.*

```
do while (database 1 is not end of file)
  read dField from database1 into date_field
  read fname from database1 into first_name
  read lname from database1 into last_name
  date_field = ConvertDateToString(date_field)
  tmp_date1 = substring(date_field, 1,6)
  tmp_date2 = substring(date_field,7,2)
  if (MakeNumber(tmp_date2) < 50)
    new_date = tmp+date1 + "20" + tmp_date2
  else
    new_date = tmp+date1 + "19" + tmp_date2
  end if
  new_date = ConvertStringToDate(new_date)
  insert new record into database2
  replace dField in database2 with new_date
  replace fname in database2 with first_name
  replace lname in database2 with last_name
end do
```

The program inserts the appropriate century digits into the date field as discussed in other listings shown in this chapter. Finally, a new record in database2 is created and each field is stored in that database. The bridge program continues executing this logic until the program encounters the end of database1.

You will find that building a bridge program is a very cost-effective way to temporarily address the year 2000 compliant problem. I emphasize the word *temporary*. A bridge program is not a permanent solution to the problem. This program only buys your firm time to fix the problem properly.

The Case of...The Forgotten Bridge Program

An employee benefits firm in New England provides various ancillary services to major corporations regarding benefits programs. The firm receives from clients information about employees, then uses this information to provide customized employee reports and analyses, which are printed and distributed to the client's employees.

The firm realized that the year 2000 bug would attack their system. So, several years ago the company decided to make their systems year 2000 compliant. They built bridge programs to restructure incoming records from client databases to conform to the firm's year 2000 compliant databases.

The firm experienced a high turnover in their technical staff, some of which was caused by the firm's diligence in addressing the year 2000 program quickly. Other firms hired away their technical employees.

A problem surfaced when a major new client started to do business with the firm. Both companies' databases were year 2000 compliant. Therefore, the technicians from the client's firm were given the file layout and told to electronically send their data.

The data was corrupted on receipt. At least that is what the firm's technicians reported to the client. They tried time and again with the same results. It was not long before higher management noticed the problem because the condition jeopardized the contract.

The culprit was the bridge program. None of the technicians in the firm realized that such a program existed. All of the data received from their other clients was not year 2000 compliant and therefore required data conversion. The new client's data was also going through this conversion process, although no conversion was necessary.

The reality about patching an existing system with a temporary program such as a bridge program is that no one ever goes back to remove the patch when a permanent repair is made to the program. Legacy systems are noted for being patchwork quilts of code that is difficult to trace.

Some firms require that programmers who build a bridge program (or a patch) place an expiration date on the program. A few companies even require bridge programs to have an automatic self-destruction mechanism. This is illustrated in Listing 5.10. However the bridge program is not actually destroyed. The program simply expires when the system date on the computer is 01/01/01. A message is displayed and the routine that corrects the date is not executed.

Of course, the drawback of incorporating a self-destruction mechanism into the logic of a bridge program is that this alarm goes off at an inappropriate moment and could easily hold up the production cycle.

Listing 5.10 Creating a bridge program with a self-destruct mechanism.

```
if (SystemDate >= 01/01/01)
   print "The bridge program is no longer active."
else
   do while (database 1 is not end of file)
    read dField from database1 into date_field
    read fname from database1 into first_name
    read lname from database1 into last_name
    date_string = ConvertDateToString(date_field)
    tmp_date1 = substring(date_string, 1, 6)
    tmp_date2 = substring(date_string,7,2)
    if (MakeNumber(tmp_date2) < 50)
       new_date = tmp_date1 + "20" + tmp_date2
    else
       new_date = tmp_date1 + "19" + tmp_date2
    end if
    new_date = ConvertStringToDate(new_date)
    insert new record into database2
    replace dField in database2 with new_date
    replace fname in database2 with first_name
    replace lname in database2 with last_name
   end do
end if
```

The Day of the Week Fix

Your system may not know the current day of the week if the system is not year 2000 compliant. The day of the week is determined by the date, including the century—and this is where the problem lies.

A system that uses a two-digit date assumes that that the century is the twentieth century. January 1, 1900, was a Monday. January 1, 2000, is a Saturday. Your system, if the twentieth century is used, is two days ahead (or four days behind) of the current day.

The key to solving this problem is with the system's date on your computer. If this date is not in compliance, then the day of the week used by your system will be wrong. However, you can easily patch your system to adjust for this error. Listing 5.11 contains a routine that determines the correct date assuming that your system's date does not use the century digits.

This routine assumes that your computer language has a function that extracts the day of the week from a date. In many languages this function is called day() and is passed a date (in this case the system's date) as an argument.

The function returns the day of the week by name. The return value from the function is then compared with known names. When a match occurs, the routine assigns the correct day to the new_day variable. Throughout the program the new_day variable is used whenever the program needs to refer to the day of the week.

Listing 5.11 Calculating the correct day of the week by name of day.

```
old_day = day(system's date)
if (old_day == Sunday)
  new_day = Friday
end if
if (old_day == Monday)
  new_day = Saturday
end if
if (old_day == Tuesday)
```

```
  new_day = Sunday
end if
if (old_day == Wednesday)
  new_day = Monday
end if
if (old_day == Thursday)
  new_day = Tuesday
end if
if (old_day == Friday)
  new_day = Wednesday
end if
if (old_day == Saturday)
  new_day = Thursday
end if
```

Some functions return a number that represents the day. Sunday is assigned the value 1 and Saturday the value 7. In Listing 5.11, I assume the name of the day is returned by the function. However, Listing 5.12 provides a similar routine that adjusts the current day if the day function returns the number of the day.

Listing 5.12 *Calculating the correct day of the week by number of day.*

```
old_day = day(system's date)
if (old_day == 1 or old_day = 2)
  new_day = old_day + 5
else
  new_day = old_day - 2
end if
```

Deciding Which Solution Is the Best Fix

Every company must come to terms with how they intend to make their systems year 2000 compliant. I covered in some detail the methods that most corporations are considering to resolve this issue. These fixes include the following:

- Change logic in programs to account for the century digits.

- Expand the size of date fields in databases.

- Modify the bits that represent the two-digit year to accommodate the four-digit year.

- Create a sliding date window that covers the span of 100-years.

- Build a bridge program to convert incompatible date formats.

Which method should you use in your firm? The answer is a mixture of these solutions. Each one of these techniques is an ideal solution for a particular situation. However, none of these methods will address every situation.

The Ideal Solution

The ideal solution is to change all the dates and data that is derived from dates (i.e., serial number) to account for the century digits. This solution requires the following steps:

- Date fields must be expanded by two-digits.

- Programs that use date fields must be adjusted to accommodate these two-digits.

- Date values stored in the data fields must be converted to the four-digit year.

However, as I pointed out throughout this chapter, there are real live problems that can prevent you from implementing the ideal solution. Fortunately, you have other techniques on which you can fall back.

No Room to Expand All Date Fields

The size of the date fields can be an obstacle, especially if there are many dates used in each record of a very large database. Remember that you do not have to expand every date field. Here is what you can do:

- Identify the date fields that are used as search criteria, sorts, and keys for index files, then expand those date fields and insert the two century digits.

- Dates that are used in calculations or in reports can be modified by code within the program without having to expand those fields in the database.

- Dates that are sent to other systems can be modified by using a bridge program.

- Dates that are received from other systems which are in the four-digit year (i.e., 1997) format can be modified to a two-digit year format (i.e., 97) by a bridge program.

Out of Time to Make the Fix

Running out of time is another real live problem that prevents you from addressing the year 2000 problem in the ideal way. There is an approach that you can use to get your firm through the rough times until all your systems are year 2000 compliant. Here is the method I suggest:

- Create a sliding window by inserting a routine, similar to the one in this chapter, in programs and read and write date data.

- Build bridge programs to send and receive data to and from other systems.

These are two typical scenarios that many companies will face when confronting the year 2000 problem. However, every company truly has a unique situation and your year 2000 team must be able to apply the proper combination of techniques to resolve the problem.

Should You Rebuild?

Faced with this seemingly insurmountable problem, you begin to wonder if the most effective and efficient way to attack this problem is to rebuild the systems from scratch. For some legacy systems, rebuilding is a viable option and very desirable.

Legacy systems are notorious for having an uncountable number of patches that make tracing the system nearly impossible. This condition complicates the effort of trying to locate all the places where dates are used in the system.

If you estimate the time and expense that will be involved to bring a legacy system in compliance with the year 2000, you might find that rebuilding is the only sound business decision. Otherwise, you will be spending good money to fix up an old wreck.

Here is an approach that is bound to keep your firm on track with the year 2000 problem and give you a brand new system and a competitive edge into the new century.

First, do not lose sight of the drop-dead deadline. Whether or not you rebuild to modify, all your systems must be ready to do business on the first business day of the twenty-first century.

I suggest that you develop two plans: a plan for rebuilding and a plan for patching. The rebuilding plan will call for reverse engineering of the existing system, then development of functional and technical specifications. In addition these plans must include any improvements in the system that the business and technical staff can identify.

The plan for patching the existing system should follow the technique that I outline above in the section "Out of Time to Make the Fix." Do as little patching as necessary to keep the system operational until the new system is in production.

The start date for work on the patches should be backed down from the drop-dead deadline. That is, the patch job may take a year before the current system is year 2000 compliant. This includes full implementation.

The drop-dead deadline is 11/01/99, therefore work should commence on 11/01/98.

Until 11/01/98, all efforts should be concentrated on rebuilding the system. If work on the new system is completed prior to 11/01/98, then the plan to patch the current system can be scrapped.

However, if the new system is not ready by 11/01/98, then work must immediately begin on patching the current system while the new system remains under construction. This parallel effort will ensure that your firm meets the drop-dead deadline either with the new system or with the patched current system. Furthermore, you are assured that shortly after the turn of the century your firm will have a brand new system.

Testing Your Solution

About 40% of the process of bringing your systems into year 2000 compliance is testing. So many programs, databases, index files, and feeds can change that testing becomes the most time-consuming part of the entire process. Most companies are required to test all of their systems, something that probably has never been undertaken in the firm.

The test scenario is rather straightforward: Change the system date to reflect a day in the year 2000, then run a normal day's processing. Watch all the systems very carefully to see if there is a malfunction and review all data output to be sure that the correct information is reported.

Hazards of Forwarding the System's Date

Now that I told you something that you could figure out yourself, let us explore some other factors that may not be so obvious. Let's begin with a review of the potential hazards of forwarding the system's date. The first problem that comes to mind is that surrounding the use of passwords.

Passwords expire based on the current system's date and the expiration date set by the system administrator. Changing the system's date to a day in the year 2000 will probably require that all passwords be reset. This includes login passwords into the system and passwords that are encoded into the system to facilitate automatic logins to other systems. In addition to passwords, data sets and user IDs might also be affected by a change in the system's date.

A more serious problem can arise with product licenses. These may be set to expire on a particular day and require a license renewal to reinstate the product. This may prevent you from conducting a full systems test. This problem is further complicated if you have only one license for the product, which prevents you from having an independent copy of the product in your test environment. Use caution if a product must be shared with the production environment. Changing the system's date could stop the product from working in production.

You must have an independent, isolated environment that mirrors production that can be used for testing. A copy of all the components used in production must be placed in the test environment. Do not share components such as data sets and licensed products. Shared components could result in failures in the production environment.

Data used for the test must contain dates that are in the twentieth and twenty-first centuries. You may want to take a representative sample of production data and modify the dates to conform with the test time period.

Set the system's date to 12/31/99 and the system's time to 11:55 P.M. then wait five minutes and start the processing cycle. Make sure that all components of the system run. Avoid assuming that the changes will not affect a particular data feed or report.

Another test is to set the system's date to 12/31/99 and the system's time to 12:01 A.M., then start the full day's processing cycle and continue directly into the next day's processing cycle. This test shows the results of running the normal schedule that overlaps the change of the century.

Here is another test that you should try. Set the system's date to 02/28/2000 and the system's clock at 11:55 P.M., then run your systems. This tests how your systems will react to the date 02/29/2000. The year 2000 is a leap year.

The Case of...The Limited Resources

A health insurer in Virginia was faced with a serious lack of resources when the time arrived to conduct a full production test of all their systems. The firm simply did not have sufficient hardware and other resources that could duplicate their production environment.

The firm had 2500 personal computers and 7000 dumb terminals connected to their mainframes. They were running about 57 key systems that contained nearly 20 million lines of code.

Their year 2000 team resolved this problem by carefully examining each system to determine the system's dependencies. They identified the resources required to run each system and identified the system's input and output feeds. They also identified the order in which the systems ran in production.

With this information, the year 2000 team scheduled the test of each system independently of the other systems where possible. This method provided a sufficient testing environment without the need to replicate the complete production environment.

Be Sure to Review...

Focus your review of the test results on the likely areas of your system that will fail if your repair does not fix the problem. One of these areas is reports that show records sorted in date order. Examine sorted data carefully to determine if the sort is accurate.

Likewise, you should query databases by date. This too should work fine. If wrong data or no data is returned, then there is a chance one or more index files are corrupted and need to be rebuilt using the newly formatted date data.

Data feeds into and from your systems must be reviewed to determine if bridge programs are working properly. You cannot assume that because a feed is transmitted successfully that the correct data is stored properly in the database. Someone must look at the data itself.

Other areas of concern are places in your systems where date calculations are performed and the routines that automatically back up and archive data. Each of these components is date sensitive and should be inspected carefully each time a test is conducted.

Systems in many corporations do not operate in isolation. This is especially true for client/server systems that connect resources across the country and around the world. A full test of such systems requires that all the components be operational and connected to the test system.

The major drawbacks of testing your systems for the year 2000 is that you cannot conduct a parallel test to ensure that proper results are produced by the new system.

Parallel testing is a traditional method of verifying that a new version of an existing system functions properly. A previous day's data is input into the new system. The output of the previous day's processing from the current system is then compared—many times electronically—to the output of the new system. If the output is the same, then the new system is ready for production. However, parallel testing cannot be performed with the year 2000 compliance test because the current system cannot properly process data that contains dates beyond the twentieth century. There is no output from the current system that can be compared to the output of the new system.

Therefore, year 2000 compliance testing takes longer to perform than traditional testing. Each piece of output data must be manually reviewed to determine if the system is working properly. Likewise, dates in databases and in data feeds must also be manually examined. There is no shortcut that can be used in year 2000 compliance testing.

However, you can use sophisticated software tools that help to automate some of the testing procedures. You will read more about these software tools later in this book.

The Case of ... A Lot of Testing

A California financial services firm found that year 2000 compliance testing was the most difficult aspect of modifying their systems. The company provides factoring services to retailers around the world. Retailers used the firm's computerized purchasing system to allow customers to avoid paying cash for purchases. The company kept 3% of the purchase price as payment for the service.

There are 35 million lines of code in the company's computerized purchasing system. Each line of code had to be tested in a simulation of the firm's global production environment.

The firm's year 2000 team spent two months developing the comprehensive test plan. Six months were necessary to complete the test of the new system. The test simulated the change of date into the next century and the effect the date 02/29/2000 had on the system.

Furthermore, their test required global participation that included any effect that the time zone changes combined with the turn of the century had on the new system. This was a massive undertaking that required about 100 managers and technicians to work 15-hour days and sometimes around the clock to account for the times zone differences.

Implementing Your Plan

You are in the home stretch. All your systems are fixed and your quality assurance staff tells you that unit testing and complete systems tests are completed. The next step is to place all the new systems and databases into production. Time has come to start the engine and see if your systems run.

You would think after all this effort that implementing the systems would be the simplest task in the entire project. Unfortunately nothing is simple when you tackle the year 2000 problem.

Placing a system in production is not a new procedure for your system's department. This process occurs often in the course of business.

However, this implementation is drastically different than the normal routine since all of your systems and databases are placed in production at the same time.

Implementation requires planning. Many factors must be addressed to ensure that the implementation process flows smoothly. The first factor to consider is timing. When can you physically move all the year 2000 compliant systems and database into the production environment?

Before you rush to answer this question, you must ask several other questions:

- How long does it take the technical staff to make this move?
- How long does it take to prepare the production environment for the new systems?
- How long does it take to perform a cursory test of the system in the production environment?
- What time period is the least disruptive to business operations?
- What data feeds from other systems must be available when the move is made into production?

Ideally the implementation begins at the first opportunity after testing is completed and long before the turn of the century. Most firms begin this process at the close of business on a Friday or on the eve of a four-day holiday. This period gives all your technicians time to complete the implementation process without the imminent pressure of the start of business.

Special care must be taken to ensure that the data in the new databases is current and expunged of test data before the databases are moved into the production environment. Remember, when your systems are activated, they will be processing production data.

Use a checklist to help organize the move. This list must contain all the components that are necessary to operate your production systems. The list is checked as each component is moved from the test environment to the production environment. Components also include data feeds coming into the systems and data feeds that are being sent to other systems.

Once you are satisfied that all the components are in production, you can turn the switch and start the new systems. If possible, attempt to process data to see if all systems are working properly.

Be sure to review critical areas of the system. These are places where you can tell if date conversion is working such as in reports that are generated by the system.

An alternative to fully testing the system in the production environment is to carefully monitor the output of daily processing by the new system during the first few weeks of operation. Pay careful attention to the critical areas of the system.

What may be the most important aspect of any implementation plan is the development of a contingency plan in case a major component of a system fails in production. Decide now, before you begin implementation, about how you intend to recover if each of the systems fails to process data properly.

Help and the Toolbox

The job of bringing your systems in compliance with the year 2000 is an enormous undertaking that requires countless hours from management and staff to accomplish the goal. Where do you begin? How can you make sure the problem is being addressed in the most efficient way?

Earlier in this book, you learned the answer to this first question. Start by assembling the right talent into a year 2000 team, then follow up with a methodical approach to identify and resolve issues that impede your systems from being in compliance.

The answer to the second question is for your year 2000 team to get help from outside vendors and consultants, and to use tools that can increase the speed at which your staff can work. You can also receive information from locations on the World Wide Web. You will find Web sites to be a key element in your staff's continuing education about potential problems and their resolutions.

In this chapter, we explore where you can get help and the tools that you should consider for your toolbox. More than 50 vendors are waiting to take on all or part of your year 2000 compliance problem as their problem. Furthermore, more than 90 software tools await your consideration. Some of these tools help you manage the entire project. Other tools help technicians sift through all your code. Some of the tools generate code for your staff.

Throughout this chapter we will profile a few of the vendors who specialize in solving the year 2000 compliance problem and a few tools you should consider purchasing for your toolbox.

What Kind of Help Do You Need?

Before you rush to assemble a team of high-priced consultants to fix your year 2000 problems and buy every tool in sight, stop! Determine specifically what problems lie ahead and what talent or tool is required to address the problem. Look in house first to decide if the talent is already on staff or the tool is already in your toolbox.

Say that you are in need of someone who knows an obscure assembly language that was popular decades ago, but has since been replaced by more modern languages.

The instinctive approach is to call consulting firms who might have a person with that talent on staff. Remember the skunk facing down the Mack truck? The natural reaction may not be the most appropriate action. In this situation, the year 2000 team should review the personnel folders and/or resumes of the current technical staff.

Technicians on staff have many skills—probably more skills than those they were hired to perform. An assumption made by many technical managers is that the only skills possessed by their technical staff are the skills they use to do their current jobs. This is a false assumption.

Examine the background of your entire technical staff to elicit information about the skilled technicians that you might already have at your fingertips—possibly at a more favorable cost to the firm than that of an outside consultant. Once they are found, reassign these staff members to the project.

Another condition that causes the year 2000 team to panic—and stop thinking logically—is when source code cannot be found. How can the source code be regenerated? This question pops to mind first. However, the first question should be "Did we look in all the possible places to find the source code?" The answer to this question is typically no. Many firms search through all the disks and tapes that are currently available on the system to track down the source code files. But that is where the search ends. Not many firms investigate their archive files, which are probably stored in a remote location. In many firms, the technical staff backs up all the programs and data every day and places them in storage. These files remain in storage for nearly a decade or more and are forgotten.

A few days of searching the archives could be well spent especially if you find the source code. These few days could save months of work that would have been spent recreating the source code file.

Countless problems confront a firm that attempts to bring its systems into year 2000 compliance. For each problem, management of the firm must decide whether or not the problem can be resolved with in-house staff. This is usually the least expensive approach, although this method does interfere with the staff's regular assignments.

Once a list of problems is assembled and a determination is made that the problem cannot be resolved internally, then alternative solutions can be evaluated. Various techniques can be employed:

- An outside firm can be hired to bring the firm into compliance without the use of the internal staff.

- An outside manager or consulting firm can be brought in to manage your in-house staff.

- An inside management team can be assembled to manage an outside team of technicians.

- The internal staff is used for the entire project, except when special skills are necessary. In such a case, a consultant is brought in to provide this special help.

Various combinations of in-house staff and consultants can be used to assemble the talent that is necessary to resolve all the problems you face during this project. No one combination of talents can fix all the systems in your firm.

Instead, each system must be addressed independently of the other systems and a team formed to attack each problem associated with fixing the system. In many situations, the same team can move from one system to another. However, there will be occasions when the composite of the team must change and be enhanced with special skills.

A word of caution: The security of your firm's systems will be breached once outside staff is brought in to help you fix the year 2000 problem. This is especially true if the outside staff must sift through all your systems to identify where dates are used in the system.

Many firms require outside firms and their staff to sign nondisclosure statements that place legal restrictions on outside firms and their employees. However, this really does not stop anyone from using the knowledge gained by snooping through your systems on future assignments. You really cannot prevent this breach of security from occurring.

You can reduce the opportunity for your system to "walk" away with the outside firm by restricting their staff's access to your resources. Here are some techniques to consider:

- Do not allow the outside staff the capability to make electronic copies of the system. Where possible, they should use dumb terminals or computers that do not have access to a floppy disk.

- Prevent electronic file transfer to outside the firm. They should not be allowed access to the Internet or any telephone line that can be used to connect to the outside world. Pay careful attention to fax lines since these lines could be unplugged and plugged into a portable computer.

- Do not allow the outside staff to print lines of code. If they cannot print, they cannot walk away with a printed copy of your system.

- Create a room where the outside staff can work. Place lockers or personal storage space outside of the room where the outside staff can put their personal belongings. Do not allow anything to be brought into the room where changes are to be made to your system. The policy should be "nothing is carried into the room, and nothing is carried out of the room."

Where to Get Advice

Some people may agree with the old saying that "free advice is not worth the price that you pay for it." This is not always true, especially if you search for help on the Internet. There are a number of places on the Internet where information about the year 2000 problems and possible solutions are discussed.

Here are some sites that you can review for additional information about the year 2000 problem and to see how the cyberspace community is solving problems similar to yours.

Web Sites

The Year 2000 Information Center

    http://www.year2000.com

IBM

    http://www.software.ibm.com

A Collection Of References

    http://www.club.innet.be/~janjedsp/y2k.htm

Mailing Lists and Newsletters

Discussions of Year 2000

    Send e-mail to listmanager@hookup.net with SUBSCRIBE
    YEAR2000 as the BODY of the message.

Year 2000 News, an Internet newsletter

    To subscribe, send the message "SUBSCRIBE" in the SUBJECT
    field of your e-mail to news2000 request@andrew.cais.com

The Millennium Journal

Data Dimensions, Inc.

777 108th Ave. NE, Suite 2070

Bellevue, WA 98004

Phone: 800 708-0675, 206 688-1000

Fax: 206 688-1099

E-mail: `76311.1542@compuserve.com, rbergeon@aol.com`

Tick Tick Tick, a quarterly newsletter

2000AD, Inc.

PO Box 020538, Brooklyn, NY 11202-0012,

1-800-643-TICK (8425),

Fax: 718-797-9410.

Types of Available Tools

Tools are available that can transform the laborious job of organizing the year 2000 project and analyzing the systems into manageable tasks. Tools can assist everyone associated with the project so that they may do their jobs more efficiently. Tools are divided into these general categories:

- Project management;
- Code restructuring and editing;
- Code generation; and
- System testing.

Project management software helps to schedule and track tasks that must be performed to repair a system. Project management software is used to manage resources used during the project and analyze the complexity of the job to help with estimates. This tool helps to size the project and determine resources necessary to get the job done on time.

Some project management tools enable you to slice into a system, level by level, beginning with a high-level overview of the system, then moving lower into each program and routine.

Code restructuring and editing tools enable you to quickly find lines of code that need to be changed. You can also use these tools to compare code with data files. Detailed investigations can be performed by using these tools to cross reference lines of code and data in multiple programs. The same tools can also be used to make the actual changes in the logic of the program.

If you are unable to make changes directly to the existing code or database, another option is to rebuild a piece of the system—a gigantic problem that is easily overcome through the use of code generation tools.

Code generation tools are used to create databases from data structure diagrams and reports from report generation tools. These tools make rebuilding user interfaces a snap.

Testing tools make the tedious task of testing your system as painless as possible. These are "must have" tools when you start testing all your systems at the same time. Testing tools generate and organize test data and ensure that all possible variations of data are passed through your system and used during testing. Testing tools are used both on replicated systems then on the system prior to full implementation. Testing tools simulate typical and atypical data flows into your system. You can also use these tools to automatically enter data to replicate a normal day's activities.

In addition to purchasing tools, you can also purchase ready-to-run and ready-tested date routines that are year 2000 compliant. A routine is an isolated and independent piece of code that performs a particular function. Your programs can execute routines whenever the program needs to perform the function. Say your program needs to know the number of business days that fall between two dates. The program currently calls a routine your programmers built, however, this routine is not year 2000 compliant. Instead of fixing this routine, you could buy one that is ready to go from an outside vendor. This shortens the year 2000 project since inserting the routine could take less time than fixing your own routine.

....

Selecting a Help Provider

The question that begs to be answered is "How do you acquire the services of outside vendors to help you bring your systems into compliance?" We will try to answer this question.

The first step is to determine the kind of help you require. The inventory and assessment processes help you make this determination. Next, decide if your present staff can handle the job. If not, then you require the services of an outside vendor.

The remainder of this chapter is devoted to reviewing services available to assist in the upgrading of your systems. Before reading this survey, though, you should develop a selection process. Here are some ideas that should be considered as part of this process:

- Look for firms that have had successful experiences bringing systems into compliance. Some firms want to get into this business but have no experience.

- The location of the firm should be convenient to your office. Although the actual repair can be performed over long distances through phone lines, there will be a need for personal contact on a regular basis. Vendors who are stationed a distance from your location may be willing to relocate staff closer to your site for the life of the project. However, chances are this cost is hidden in your bill.

- What is the vendor's productive staff-to-client ratio? The productive staff are the people who directly fix the problem as compared with support staff that do not work directly on your project. You should expect a team of their staff to be assigned only to your project.

- Determine the financial stability of the firm. Your accounting department can perform the necessary financial background check. In addition, you must decide whether the vendor has a sufficient cash flow to meet payroll and bills for three months without depending on your cash payment. There have been occasions when vendors fail to pay their employees—the guys who are actually fixing your system.

- Establish your expectations before looking at vendors. Create a list of tasks you expect a vendor to perform for your firm. Besides the obvious list of tasks, be sure to include regular meetings, status reports, and everything else you normally require of your own staff.

- Make sure the vendor you choose specializes in your operating system or computer system.

Invite all vendors to submit their offers in writing. Compare these to your list of criteria to narrow the list to a few likely candidates. Interview the candidates to further reduce the list to two or three vendors.

Once the number of candidates has been refined, you should begin the due diligence process. The *due diligence process* is a thorough background check. Everything produced in writing by a vendor or claims made by the vendor must be confirmed by your firm. This is a long and detailed process, so you should only conduct such an investigation on those candidates with whom you are ready to begin negotiations. If any vendor balks about the due diligence processing, eliminate the vendor from contention.

The due diligence process separates truth from fiction. If a vendor lies to you now, how can you trust the vendor to fix your mission critical system? This process provides information with which you can begin to formulate a strategy for negotiation.

Your staff has probably negotiated with vendors for many services purchased by your company. The negotiation process with year 2000 vendors is very much the same process as you follow today. However, here are some tips that you should consider:

- Address each system individually. List what you expect the vendor to do for each system.

- The vendor must commit to assigning a minimum number of administrative and productive staff to each system and to the project.

- Milestones must be agreed on and a penalty clause instituted if a substantial number of milestones are missed.

- Payment should be made only as each system becomes compliant. No progress payment should be made.

- Any resource supplied by your firm should reduce the price of fixing the system. You should receive credit for providing office space and computer facilities.

- Agree on which, if any, code becomes common code to be shared with the vendor's other customers. You may be able to have parts of the system rebuilt free of charge if the vendor can resell the code to another customer. In some situations, vendors encourage customers to share code. There is no price reduction, but you get a chance to use other customer's code at no cost to you.

- Be sure your agreement identifies who owns the code and who has the right to change the code. You should retain all rights.

- A performance bond could be required in some situations. A performance bond requires the vendor to make arrangements with an insurance company to pay you a specific amount of money in case the vendor does not complete the job.

Your attorney and managers of your computer department can enhance this list.

Offshore Service Providers

As you read the next section, which contains a partial list of firms that specialize in helping clients bring their systems in compliance with the twenty-first century, you will notice these suppliers are based throughout the world.

The thought of using an offshore firm to provide domestic technology services might seem absurd. Why would any firm pack up their software electronically and place it on a plane bound for a foreign land when the same service can be provided at home at their own facilities?

Until a few years ago, the concept of using a foreign company to develop software did not make much sense. However, recent developments in satellite communications have made using offshore operations a viable alternative to building or fixing software at home.

A misconception many have about offshore operations is that your systems must reside on their computers for you to use their services. This is not true. Programmers and other technicians based practically anywhere in the world can use their terminals to connect to your computer via telephone lines and satellites. The result is like having these programmers on your site, except you do not have to provide office space, parking, and terminals. Furthermore, you can have a wide variety of technicians with many skills at your disposal.

Another misconception is security. How can you be sure your systems are safe when they are being worked on by programmers hundreds of miles away from your location? Security depends on the methods currently being used to keep your systems safe. Foreign programmers look like any of your own programmers to your computers. Programmers must provide the appropriate identification and passwords to gain access to your systems. And their IDs are typically limited to areas of your systems where access is necessary to complete their assignments. The same is true for foreign programmers.

Some firms that use offshore services build a firewall between foreign operations and their computers. Programmers based abroad can only connect to the firewall computer, which in turn connects to computers that run your main system. So even if outside programmers were to circumvent your security scheme, they would only be able to poke around the firewall computer, which should not allow access to any of your systems.

Still another concern about using offshore service providers is the expense. Satellite links and long-distance phone calls for hours at a time are very expensive. However, this expense is typically offset by the hourly fee paid to the offshore provider.

Local wages and facility costs may be dramatically lower in foreign locations. This means the cost of quality programmers is not nearly as high as similar costs domestically. The dramatic cost savings offsets the communications link costs and still results, at times, in overall cost savings for domestic corporations.

There are drawbacks to using offshore vendors. First of all, domestic companies may face repercussions by sending the work abroad instead of using the domestic workforce. Negative publicity can hinder the operations of your business well beyond the cost savings realized by sending the work offshore.

Then there is the lack of control that domestic firms normally feel they have over vendors. Clients cannot simply drop by the vendor to see their operations. Although many offshore vendors have domestic offices, these are staffed mainly by sales personnel and system analysts. All of their technical people may be based abroad.

Be cautious when performing due diligence on offshore operations. In some cases, you will not be able to find all the information about the firm that you can about domestic firms. Disclosure laws in foreign countries are different than they are for domestic firms.

In addition, you must determine if the offshore firm is really a general contractor rather than a direct employer of the programmers who are fixing your systems. There have been situations where the local office in the United States is operated by a foreign national who portrays his company as being a substantial multinational service provider. In reality, his company is a sales agent for a loosely knit organization of small, foreign software houses, some of which your firm would not normally do business with—even if they were based domestically. Unfortunately there is no sure way to know the relationship between your domestic contact and the people actually doing the work except to visit all the sites yourself.

You must be careful in selecting what software is electronically shipped abroad should you decide to have the offshore vendor use their facilities rather than yours. Government regulations might prevent you from sending software with certain encryption algorithms abroad without prior permission from the State Department.

Furthermore, you may not have the right to distribute copies of third-party software to the foreign vendor. This includes libraries used by your systems. However, both of these restrictions are probably avoided by having the offshore vendor's programmer connect directly to your computers so that the software never leaves your computer.

So should you consider using the services of an offshore vendor? The advantages include:

- Cost savings;

- A very broad pool of talent; and

- Quick expansion of your facilities. Many offshore operations have their own facilities equipped with both old and new technology platforms that can be used should you decide to ship (electronically) your systems to their location.

There are, of course, disadvantages also:

- Negative publicity for shipping domestic jobs abroad;
- Problems finding necessary information during the due diligence process;
- The feeling of less control over the vendor; and
- No legal right to ship all or parts of your software abroad.

Help Providers

A list of vendors follows who specialize in helping firms address the year 2000 problem. This list is not inclusive; it is merely a representative sample of vendors who provide tools and other services. You can use this list as a starting point to begin your selection process.

INTERSOLV
800-547-4000
www.intersolv.com

Product: Tools; consulting services

INTERSOLV offers tools that help you in the change management process, the process of moving the old system out and a new system into production. They call their group of tools the Year 2000 Solution.

At the heart of the Year 2000 Solution is the Maintenance Workbench, which provides an environment for researching software and changing software. The Maintenance Workbench is designed for team use and works in a client/server environment.

Another key component of the Year 2000 Solution is the PVCS Series. This series contains software that enforces programming standards in your code and tracks changes made to the code. In addition, components of the PVCS Series are used to help you organize and control changes made to your software.

Each component of the Year 2000 Solution is designed to be used in each phase of your year 2000 project. For example, the Maintenance Workbench produces an Application Portfolio Assessment Report that contains all the information gathered during the inventory and assessment phase of the project.

This information is then used to group related tasks into work units and into a full work plan for the project. This all takes place within the Maintenance Workbench environment.

As the focus of the project moves from planning to changing the software, information generated by the Maintenance Workbench is then transferred to the PVCS Tracker component of the Year 2000 Solution.

Tracker records the life of each change to the system. Changes are entered into Tracker, then assigned to a technician. Everything that affects the task such as a modification of the functional or technical specifications is recorded by Tracker. Tracker also produces a standard set of status reports to help the whole Year 2000 team keep up with the entire project.

The Maintenance Workbench also plays a critical role in the modification of your software by your technicians. You can link your own tools such as editors, compilers, and debuggers directly to the Maintenance Workbench. This permits your programmers to call these other tools directly from the Maintenance Workbench.

The Year 2000 Solution also comes with a safety net called PVCS Version Manager. This tool acts like a traffic cop for your source code. The Version Manager manages multiple revisions of your software and stops programmers from inadvertently overwriting versions of the software. Your programmers will not lose their work. Best of all, the Version Manager can be directly linked to the Maintenance Workbench.

INTERSOLV also provides consultants to help you work through your year 2000 problem. They call this service ServiceDirect, and their staff uses a proven year 2000 development model to make sure your systems are compliant in time for the first business day of the new century.

Trans Century Data Systems
  800-837-7989

Product: Date routines

Trans Century Data Systems has been providing solutions to date-related problems since 1989 when they developed routines that fixed a client's single-digit year problem. Throughout the 1980s their client used 0 through 9 to represent the year. This was not a problem until 1990, but Trans Century Data Systems came to their rescue to adjust all the date calculations.

Trans Century Data Systems then developed a set of calendar routines that could be called by a client's program. This ensures that dates are properly constructed and that calculations are compliant with the year 2000. These routines can be called wherever the client's program performs a date calculation.

Their date routines are well known in the industry for being accurate and portable across platforms. These routines can be used for mainframe, workstation, and personal computer applications. They work with LE-379, CICS, ADS/O, IMB, DB2, OS/VS COBOL, COBOL II, and COBOL 370.

Compatibility of routines across platforms is critical to a firm whose systems run in various environments. The firm is assured that all the date calculations are performed the same way and produce the same results.

Furthermore, time is saved during the year 2000 project since the date routines supplied by Trans Century Data Systems need only be tested once, separately from the systems. Knowing that these routines work relieves the staff from repeatedly testing the same routine for each system.

Trans Century Data Systems' date routines are used in a variety of industries such as retailing, pharmaceuticals, banking, and insurance. The routines can handle 100 different date formats including Gregorian, Julian, Lilian, right or left justified, zero or space filled, formatted or unformatted, and with or without century values.

These routines also support the date formats required by ANSI, DB2, CICS, and AS400 which makes the Trans Century Data Systems routines a product that should be considered if you want to avoid building or upgrading your own date routines.

Andersen Consulting
888-594-3577

Product: Consulting services

Andersen Consulting provides a complete solution to a firm's year 2000 problem. The firm's method is to help the client over the major hurdle of bringing their systems into year 2000 compliance. Once this obstacle is overcome, Andersen Consulting seeks to leverage their solution into a longer term strategy for the client.

Instead of approaching the year 2000 problem in isolation, Andersen Consulting tries to use this situation as an impetus to review the overall business and system strategy of the client. This is a different approach than those used by other consulting firms who remain focused solely on the year 2000 project.

Andersen Consulting approaches the client's problem by conducting a full review of all systems. All system, database, and related files are inventoried using methods developed by Andersen Consulting over decades of work to address systems problems for major firms.

Still using these proven techniques, Andersen Consulting assesses the client's systems to determine the system's value to the client and the strategic role the systems play in the client's business.

The assessment process, of course, determines the impact the year 2000 problem has on each system. Furthermore, an analysis is made to determine the cost of bringing the system into compliance as compared with the system's residual value.

Andersen Consulting does not blindly recommend fixing the current system. In some situations, the best solution is to rebuild the system that will address the year 2000 problem and address the long-term business of the client. The year 2000 problem gives clients the opportunity to bring legacy systems into the twenty-first century—including the use of new technology.

This value-added benefit of bringing legacy systems into compliance is a stronghold for Andersen Consulting. Andersen Consulting has broad experience addressing all kinds of systems-related problems for clients.

This places Andersen Consulting in the unique position of being able to quickly change old systems over to new technology.

With these changes Andersen Consulting implements a systems maintenance methodology that, if followed by the client, will ensure that the systems are organized for any changes in the future.

KPMG Peat Marwick LLP
617-988-1060

Product: Consulting services

KPMG Peat Marwick looks at the year 2000 problem from the viewpoint of both a technologist and a CPA. The technologist inventories a client's system and makes an assessment of the effect the year 2000 problem has on the system. However, instead of simply determining if the system needs to be upgraded for the year 2000, KPMG Peat Marwick decides if a rewrite or a package solution is the best solution. Depending on the need, KPMG Peat Marwick sends in an appropriate team to resolve the problem.

The firm's World Class IT Enabling Technologies & Advanced Solutions team tackles the task of rewriting existing systems to bring them into compliance with the year 2000. They are ready to modify the existing system or, if need be, recreate the system from scratch.

However, a more economical approach might be to purchase a system that is already built and tested. This is called a *packaged system*. If this is a desired solution, then KPMG Peat Marwick calls in their Enterprise Package Solutions team.

This team uses packages such as SAP, Peoplesoft, JD Edwards, and Dun & Bradstreet to produce the same results as existing ones but without having to write a lot of code.

Once the changes are implemented, KPMG Peat Marwick uses their proprietary Global Test Methodology. This technique tests all the client's systems without disrupting the client's business. KPMG Peat Marwick uses the firm's independent verification and validation method to ensure that all systems are operational before any of them are placed into production.

As a side benefit that is important for public corporations, the complete year 2000 upgrade is supervised by a Big 6 CPA firm — KPMG Peat Marwick. KPMG Peat Marwick is in a position to certify that all the systems are in compliance for the year 2000.

ISOGON

800-568-8828

Product: Tools

ISOGON produces an important software tool, called SoftAudit, that helps to inventory all MVS systems. This product searches through all your systems and related source code to load modules in production. Furthermore, SoftAudit indicates the size of each program by lines of code.

SoftAudit does not solve the year 2000 program for your firm. Instead, SoftAudit provides the information you need to develop a year 2000 plan and prioritize the repair of each system.

An advantage of using SoftAudit is that it tells you about applications that are on your production system but are not used. Not only does this information cut down on wasted development time (no need to fix a program that is not being used) but this information also enables you to remove the program from production, thereby freeing resources.

Another critical piece of information supplied by SoftAudit is who uses each of your applications. SoftAudit identifies applications by user IDs. At first this benefit does not seem obvious. However, this information helps you identify which business units in your firm use the system. Your year 2000 team can then contact those business units to investigate how date calculations in the system influence business operations. There is no need to guess how dates affect your business—and possibly guess wrong. SoftAudit basically tells you the business units that are affected, and who to talk to in the business unit so that you can make a proper assessment.

So, if you have any MVS systems that could be affected by the year 2000 problem, you should consider consulting SoftAudit.

Compuware Corporation
800-521-9353
www.compuware.com

Product: Tools; consulting services

Compuware is a worldwide provider of products that make programmers more productive when tackling the year 2000 problem. Their suite of tools provides a common sense method for making your systems year 2000 compliant. These tools help in analyzing the impact the year 2000 problem has on your systems and then assists with implementing those changes. You will find that these tools ensure your new systems are thoroughly tested.

Compuware's suite of tools includes File-AID, XPEDITER+, PATHVU, and XPEDITER/Xchange. File-AID helps you to maintain consistency in managing data and editing data by providing standard formats for data in your source code.

Changing and unit testing of lines of code in your system is a tedious job that is made easier to perform by using the XPEDITER and XPEDITER+ tools. These tools allows a programmer to step through lines of a program interactively to see how the code currently functions. Once the programmers discover a line of code affected by the year 2000 problem, the programmer can make the change in the source code without leaving these tools. The programmer can then step through the code again to see what effect the changes had on the operation of the program.

PLAYBACK and Hiperstation are two tools produced by Compuware that fully automate the testing process of your systems. In addition, you can establish controlled checkpoints during the testing process to test the quality of the new system.

You can expect that your present staff may become overwhelmed by the job of making your system year 2000 compliant. Compuware is ready to assist you. In addition to providing industry strengthening tools, Compuware has a professional services group on hand to take over a part or all of the task of bringing your systems up to date.

EDS
>   800-566-9337
>   www.eds.com

Product: Consulting services

EDS is a worldwide consulting firm who looks to help your firm fix the year 2000 problem and develop a strategy so your systems can support your business into the next century.

EDS has a unique approach to addressing the year 2000 problem for your firm. Their initial step is to create a Year 2000 Enterprise Leadership Team. This is a group consisting of your staff and their consultants that establishes the organization that will lead your efforts to make sure your systems become year 2000 compliant.

The Year 2000 Enterprise Leadership Team is at the helm making sure there is a clear focus for the project and the necessary authorizations to carry out the plan. Next in the command structure is the Core Project Management Team.

The Core Project Management Team is responsible for management of the day-to-day affairs of the project. This includes inventorying the systems, assessing the effect of the year 2000 on those systems, developing a plan for bringing the systems into compliance, and making, testing, and implementing the repairs.

A critical part of the EDS strategy is to establish ownership of each system in your firm. The system's owner is responsible for making the change and monitoring the progress of the change. Although in many cases members of your staff have ownership of each system, EDS is prepared to supply consultants who will take over that responsibility during the year 2000 project.

EDS also makes sure lines of communication are open between your firm and your vendors to ensure that data feeds will be in compliance in time for the year 2000. A complete assessment is also made to determine if systems operated by affiliates and vendors will have an adverse effect on your operations even if data is not exchanged between your firms.

EDS also provides risk management services that help your executives assess the exposure to your firm and your systems by the year 2000 problem. In addition, EDS is prepared to help you develop contingency plans to lessen a negative impact on you in case your systems are not in compliance in time for the new century.

EDS is a leader in projects that are large, technology intensive, time critical, and global in scope, which makes EDS a perfect candidate to fix your year 2000 problem.

KEANE Inc.
800-239-0296

Product: Outsourcing services; consulting services

KEANE Inc. is ready to assist clients with all aspects of their systems. This includes sending in a team to help manage your year 2000 program and, if clients desire, to take over all their systems in an outsourcing arrangement.

One of KEANE Inc.'s major success stories is Sears, Roebuck and Co. Sears hired KEANE Inc. to assess bringing Sears' network of information systems into compliance for the year 2000. KEANE Inc. helped Sears develop a reengineering plan that ensured they were on the right road to meeting the drop-dead deadline.

KEANE Inc. begins with what they call Enterprise Planning. This is the first phase of their methodology in which their staff and the client's staff gather information about the client's systems. Once the information is in hand, KEANE Inc.'s team focuses on understanding the client's situation. This includes learning about the client's environment; the computer languages that are used in the client's systems; databases that are used by these systems; plans for new applications and enhancements to the current systems; and the potential problems the client is facing.

KEANE Inc. divides the year 2000 problem into two critical levels. This technique enables them and their client to approach the year 2000 problem very systematically. Each level enables the team to stay focused on a piece of the problem they can solve, rather than trying to addressing every aspect of the problem at the same time.

The first level is the enterprise level. The enterprise level is where the overall year 2000 problem for clients is broken down into subprojects that are easier to manage. The second level is the technical problem-solving level. This level is where the small teams of technicians dig into the individual problems of each system and database, then make the necessary changes to bring the systems and databases into compliance.

The backbone of KEANE Inc.'s strategy is the Resolve 2000's project management structure. This concept makes the project plan flexible, similar to a high-rise building that can bend in the wind without collapsing. The year 2000 plan evolves from the current and ongoing needs of the business since business requirements may change during the course of the project.

KEANE Inc. makes sure all components of the year 2000 solution undergo a thorough cost–value analysis, and there is a contingency plan in place to address any negative events that may occur during the year 2000 project such as an unexpected situation that forces a change in priorities or a failure to maintain the current project schedule.

KEANE Inc. employs VIASOFT Inc.'s Enterprise 2000SM tool set, which automates many of the tedious steps that must be taken to survey the client's existing systems. The combination of using the right tools and a proven methodology places KEANE Inc. in the pool of candidates who can help your firm get ready for the year 2000.

SPR

  800-SPR-6651

Product: Consulting services

SPR is a large Midwestern consulting firm specializing in mainframe technology. In fact, SPR is the thirteenth largest firm in the Chicago area according to Crains Chicago Business, a regional business publication.

SPR started to develop solutions to the year 2000 problem back in 1987 when they reengineered an application to be year 2000 compliant, an application that used dates into the next century a decade ago.

The ability of SPR to tackle tough mainframe applications has made them the fancy of 17 of the largest (MVS is an IBM operations environment) users in the Midwest, most of whom use SPR to bring their MVS systems in compliance for the next century.

SPR uses a three-pronged approach to solve the year 2000 problem. They first use a staff of skilled technicians who know how to approach the problem and how to make the necessary technical repairs to a system in the shortest amount of time. The second prong is SPR's ability to motivate their clients' staff into moving from being frozen with fright into a full-fledged counterattack that cannot fail. Motivating people and keeping them motivated during a long project is a critical factor in the success of the project. The last prong is the use of the proper tools and methodology to make all aspects of the project flow smoothly. SPR uses tools like ADPAC and VIASOFT.

SPR is able to fix the year 2000 problem with a deliberate approach that quickly builds their client's confidence in them. Once the project is under way, clients are usually free to handle normal business operations since SPR has taken ownership of their year 2000 problem.

The counterattack used by SPR normally begins with creating a high—level organization within the firm—the year 2000 team—that can address the readiness issues critical to the project.

Next, SPR divides the enterprise into many upgrade units. The staff of each unit can address an independent part of the overall project. This allows many smaller projects to be under way at the same time. SPR has even, at times, recommended that upgrade units be broken into two shifts to maximize the use of technology resources.

A very important feature of SPR is their training program. At this point in time, very few technical schools are training mainframe programmers because firms have downsized mainframes. However, SPR has their own training program that can take staff trained in other disciplines and give them the mainframe skills needed to fix the year 2000 problem.

SPR encourages insourcing. *Insourcing* is the process of assembling a client's staff into a team to address the year 2000 problem. Many of SPR's year 2000 project teams are composed of about 25% of the client's own staff. This, combined with SPR's approach to the year 2000 problem, places SPR at the heart of the competition for your firm's business.

VIASOFT

> 602-952-0050
> www.viasoft.com

Product: Tools; consulting services; outsourcing services

VIASOFT has assembled products and services to address the year 2000 problem which they call the Enterprise 2000 solution. The Enterprise 2000 solution has three main components.

The first component contains products that help your firm analyze, plan, and convert code from your existing system into year 2000 compliance. These products allow your staff to perform these tasks without the need for outside consulting services.

The second component involves conversion, planning, and implementation as performed by VIASOFT's own staff. Your staff can continue to work on day-to-day business without concerning themselves with the task of upgrading your systems. VIASOFT's staff handles that chore for your firm.

The last component is outsourcing services. VIASOFT is in a position to augment your current staff and is ready to take over full responsibilities for your technology. VIASOFT becomes your technology department and is responsible for bringing your system into year 2000 compliance and maintaining those systems, hardware, databases, and staff.

VIASOFT's objective is to offer clients the best solution for their business. Whether your company simply requires tools or extra hands to address a particular problem with your systems or wants someone else to handle all your system woes, VIASOFT is in a position to step in and pick up the slack.

PKS Information Services
   402-496-8500

Product: Consulting services

PKS Information Services has recently focused their attention on solving the year 2000 problem for firms in the financial, manufacturing, and telecommunications industries by using their Suite 2000 offering.

Suite 2000 consists of a number of services from which clients can choose: IMPACT 2000 Assessment, Year 2000 Project Planning Process, and Year 2000 Renovation Process.

IMPACT 2000 Assessment is designed to identify date-related data in a client's systems and determine the impact the year 2000 has on those systems. Furthermore, IMPACT 2000 Assessment also determines the effort that needs to be made to correct the problem and determines the cost of such a repair.

Year 2000 Project Planning Process uses either a client-supplied assessment or that made by IMPACT 2000 Assessment to formulate a complete project plan for fixing the systems and databases. This component of the Suite 2000 also determines whether or not a system should be reengineered, replaced, or moved to a better platform. All of these decisions are made with the client's current and long-term business objectives in mind.

In the Year 2000 Renovation Process, PKS Information Services provides the necessary technical staff to correct a client's systems and database to become year 2000 compliant.

PKS Information Services' approach to solving the year 2000 problem is very much like a supermarket of solutions; PKS Information Services has all of them. A client can choose to have PKS Information Services assess the impact the year 2000 problem has on their firm. A client can decide to have PKS Information Services develop the comprehensive project plan. And a client can have PKS Information Services fix the problem. Of course, a client can have PKS Information Services handle the entire year 2000 project themselves without the need to disrupt the client's staff.

Information Management Resources
813-797-7080

Product: Offshore consulting services

Information Management Resources offers a comprehensive solution to the year 2000 problem using a very cost-effective approach. This firm has built an infrastructure that links client sites to over 550 software professionals worldwide through high-speed satellite communications links. This ability to tap into Information Management Resources' international technical staff enables them to benefit from economical advantages available outside of the United States. The relatively low cost of electronically doing business abroad does not reflect adversely on the quality of the work delivered to clients.

Information Management Resources performs the full systems lifecycle of your year 2000 project. The local technicians provide client site services while technicians abroad use automation tools to analyze your systems through satellite links to your facilities. Your systems never leave your facilities.

Once they develop a detailed project plan, Information Management Resources uses their Conversion Input Packages to divide the project into manageable units. Information Management Resources' Advanced Technology Group ensures that converted programs are validated for compliance.

Furthermore, Information Management Resources on-site personnel and the client's staff are in regular contact with the offshore technical staff through videoconferencing. This ability to leverage economical conditions abroad makes Information Management Resources a viable source for a low-cost solution to your year 2000 problem.

IBS Conversions
708-990-1999

Product: Consulting services

IBS Conversions has been a leader in migration methodologies since the firm began in 1982. IBS Conversions offers clients Solution 2000, which is a combination of project management, software tools, and a strategy for making sure that all your systems, regardless of platform, become year 2000 compliant in time to do business in the next century.

IBS Conversions has a suite of customized tools that makes the task of analyzing your systems an automated process. In addition, these tools are set to convert traditional COBOL programs to native AS/400, CICS/400, CICS/6000, and CICS on HP 9000 and CICS for Digital UNIX.

IBS Conversions' staff uses these and other tools to inventory all of your databases and systems to locate areas that can cause problems in the year 2000. After the results of the inventory are analyzed by IBS Conversions' staff, their experts provide clients with solid recommendations for addressing those problems.

IBS Conversions is ready to follow through on their own recommendations and have their staff implement and test those changes and turn a completely renovated system over to your staff.

Another unique feature of IBS Conversions is that they have their own facilities in Chicago, Milwaukee, Tampa, and Norfolk which are used for the conversion process. This enables clients to continue their business operations without the year 2000 project taking up valuable production resources. All of the work, if the client requests, can be performed at IBS Conversions sites.

IBS Conversions begins most projects with a pilot project. A pilot project addresses a small aspect of a client's year 2000 problem. IBS Conversions' staff works through the entire process to make this piece of the project operational. The pilot project is designed to fine-tune the IBS Conversions methodology with the way each client's business operates. This allows IBS Conversions to be flexible in their approach, so IBS Conversions' methods blend in smoothly with each client.

IBS Conversions' approach has the discipline required to get the job done with minimal interference in the normal operation of the client's business. This is a valuable factor that makes IBS Conversions a firm to consider during your selection process.

Computer Associates
  800-434-REAL

Product: Tools; consulting services

Computer Associates has developed a road map for addressing the year 2000 problem. This is a result of successfully analyzing and correcting hundreds of millions of lines of code for clients.

The approach developed by Computer Associates is to offer solutions for systems running on MVS, VSE, personal computers, and workstations without the need to move those systems to new platforms.

Computer Associates' methodology seeks to correct any noncompliant problems with your systems within your existing environment. Computer Associates feels this provides clients with significant savings in cost and resources.

Computer Associates' date detection, analysis, and reporting tools help your firm through the first phase of your year 2000 project. These tools are used to review your systems and produces inventory reports that are used to assess the year 2000 problem on your systems.

A key result of using these tools is the impact analysis report, which is a high-level report that, among other things, projects the cost of converting your systems to year 2000 compliance.

In addition, your staff will receive another report that identifies the date-sensitive fields. This multilevel report shows, on a high level, which programs have date-sensitive fields and, on a low level, the lines of code that use these fields.

Computer Associates has tools that help you manage your integrated source code repository and help your staff perform logical analysis of each program. Other tools are used for program testing and debugging. These are important assets to your staff's toolbox since these tools generate test data automatically and perform regression testing with little effort on the part of your staff.

Computer Associates is also available to lend your firm support throughout your year 2000 project. Computer Associates has teams of personal services staff to directly participate in your project in any way you require.

James Martin & Co.
  800-248-4562

Product: Consulting services

James Martin & Co. is an international firm set up to move in and help your in-house team quickly address the year 2000 problem. James Martin & Co. employs a proven set of year 2000 tools to move through the various phases of the project efficiently and without delay.

James Martin & Co. Impact Assessment and Implementation Services include three plans. The first plan is a Business Impact Analysis. This analysis looks at your business and determines business risks and exposure your firm faces in the year 2000.

The Business Impact Analysis plan also determines the feasible alternatives available to your firm such as system upgrades or replacements. As a result of this plan, your firm will have a strategy for sequencing the upgrade projects.

The second plan involves Support Infrastructure Design. This plan determines the tools, standards, procedures, role definition, and other operational requirements for each system to be upgraded.

The third plan is the Pilot Project plan. The purpose of this plan is to validate the strategy and the infrastructure that will be used in the full development process for the year 2000 project. This is an important piece of James Martin & Co.'s strategy. The Pilot Project plan determines what part of the methodology will not work for your firm and enables James Martin & Co.'s staff to provide alternative methods before a full effort is made to upgrade your systems.

The last plan is the Implementation Plan. This plan determines how you are going to implement the changes to your system.

Your firm will find all the help you need to tackle your year 2000 problem from James Martin & Co.

CAP Gemini America
   212-944-6464

Product: Consulting services

CAP Gemini America offers their TransMillennium Services to rapidly and cost effectively implement a highly automated solution to your year 2000 problem. The TransMillennium Services are based around three key features: integrated, end-to-end methodology, smart technology, and core competence.

End-to-end methodology takes your firm through the entire process of addressing the year 2000 problem. CAP Gemini America helps your firm with assessment and strategy, system renovation, validation and testing, and full implementation.

During this process, CAP Gemini America makes recommendations regarding renovating, retiring, redeveloping, replacing, or even out-sourcing your systems. Of course, you make the final decision. However, you will know that whatever you decide will be based on solid facts that were derived by CAP Gemini America.

CAP Gemini America's smart technology is based on the firm's use of their artificial intelligence based ARCdrive tool set to automate the year 2000 compliance project. ARCdrive was designed in 1987 to manage conversions of IDMS to DB2. Now this same tool is making a counterattack against the year 2000 bug more of a cleanup operation than a battle.

ARCdrive is used in every aspect of your system including JCL, file conversions, testing data, controlling sorts, and bridging other systems. This is particularly useful in cutting down on problems traditionally associated with software development and with change management such as time used to check programs in and out and with conducting tests beyond the year 2000.

The core competence is the third component of their TransMillennium Services. *Core competence* is the term coined for the experience of CAP Gemini America's staff in fixing the year 2000 problem for your company. Their staff is in a unique position to take over your problem, make the necessary repairs, and fully implement your new compliant systems. This makes CAP Gemini America a firm to consider when looking for outside help.

ADPAC Corporation
  416-777-5400
  ussyv001@ibmmail.com

Product: Tools

ADPAC Corporation used their more than 30 years of experience providing mainframe software to develop their SystemVision YEAR 2000 product. SystemVision YEAR 2000 is used to analyze, plan, and implement year 2000 date conversions in mainframe systems.

The SystemVision YEAR 2000 tool can locate all the occurrences of dates in your systems and clearly identify the exact locations in your source code that use dates. Furthermore, this tool determines how each date is defined, transferred, used on the screen, and used in calculations.

ADPAC Corporation built the SystemVision YEAR 2000 tool using unsurpassed data and logic passing technology. This ensures that no line of code that uses dates is overlooked.

Once the complete metric analysis is performed using the SystemVision YEAR 2000 tool, each application is given a difficulty rating based on the complexity of the program, the cost involved in changing the program, and the significance the program has on the operation of your business.

The SystemVision YEAR 2000 tool is one of the few products that calculates the cost estimate for making each system 2000 compliant. This tool also produces customized reports that use your own cost estimates for the projects. This is a perfect way of performing "what if" analyses.

Based on the results reported by the SystemVision YEAR 2000 tool, you can establish a priority for repairing systems and decide whether or not you will attempt the repair in house or call in a consulting firm to take over the project.

If you do decide to tackle the job yourself, then your staff will find the SystemVision YEAR 2000 tool a very useful assistant. This tool enables your programmers to step through each program, date field at a time. Changes to the code are made by pointing to the line of code, then clicking the mouse button. The SystemVision YEAR 2000 tool calls ISPF and runs customized ISPF macros that automatically replace the affected code with year 2000 compliant code.

One of ADPAC Corporation's success stories is Federal Express' which needed to sift through 100 million lines of code in a diverse multilanguage environment. This is one of the largest year 2000 projects ever attempted. Be sure to include ADPAC on your short list of tool suppliers.

ALYDAAR Software Corporation
704-544-0092

Product: Tools; consulting services

ALYDAAR Software Corporation has an artificial intelligence reengineering system that cuts down the time programmers need to search and analyze each line of code in all of your systems. They call this system SmartCode.

SmartCode "walks" through every line of code used to run your systems to first identify the software as part of your inventory, then to determine if the line of code is date sensitive.

This software does not simply record the fact that the line of code uses a date. SmartCode also records the characteristics of the date such as format and whether or not the date is used in calculations or displayed on the screen. Based on the date characteristics, SmartCode evaluates whether or not the line of code is negatively affected by the year 2000 problem, and if so what solution is best for fixing the problem.

A most interesting feature of SmartCode is that this tool adapts to your software design and standards. You can even include your own format and style guide, which is referenced by SmartCode.

SmartCode also understands any computer language including variations in languages. Code written in a dialect of COBOL, for example, will not hinder SmartCode's operation. This includes embedded code of one language (say, assembler) found in the body of the code written in another language (say, COBOL).

Although ALYDAAR Software Corporation's SmartCode is a valuable asset to any systems department, ALYDAAR Software Corporation also provides a team of technicians that is ready to help you reengineer your systems. Your year 2000 problem is nearly solved with one call to the ALYDAAR Software Corporation.

Mastech Corporation
800-311-1970

Product: Consulting services

Mastech Corporation is a global service provider with more than 1500 technicians strategically stationed throughout the world to help multinational corporations upgrade their systems to do business by the next century.

One of the major advantages of Mastech Corporation is their ability to take on projects using their own facilities. They have the manpower, hardware capacity, and office space to bring your year 2000 project into their facilities, thereby minimizing the effect of the project on your operations.

Mastech Corporation has three Indian offshore development facilities that are completely fitted with IBM and VAX mainframes, personal computers, and workstations. Your system can easily be temporarily transferred to their facilities over satellite links.

Mastech Corporation has been around since 1986 and has provided solutions to 400 of the Fortune 1000 companies.

Quintic Systems
800-699-1169

Product: Tools; consulting services

Quintic Systems developed software that attacks the year 2000 problem head on. Quintic Systems offers two key software packages: source conversion analysis and automatic file conversion.

The source conversion analysis software consists of a repository generator, extensive reporting tools, an independent analyzer, tracking capabilities, and cross referencing.

The automatic file conversion software performs file analysis, file conversion, and simulates test data among other valuable features.

Quintic Systems products works with COBOL on OS/MVS, VSE/ESA, Tandem, and Unisys; BAL assembler; PL/1; FORTRAN; APS; and fourth-generation languages such as SAS and Mark IV. In addition, their tools work with DB2, IDMS, IMS, and Oracle.

Quintic Systems also offers clients a staff ready to conduct an inventory of programs and data; assess the impact the year 2000 has on the client; develop a pilot project; and use their customized software to bring all the systems into year 2000 compliance.

Prince Software
  800-934-2022

Product: Tools; consulting services

Prince Software produces the PORTAL 2000 group of products that makes fighting the year 2000 problem less time consuming and tedious for your programmers. This group of products includes SURVEY 2000, TRANSLATE 2000, and SIMULATE 2000.

SURVEY 2000 is a tool that performs impact analysis and cross referencing on all of your systems. This tool is able to analyze COBOL, PL/1, and assembler programs to determine how dates are used.

By using parsing routines, SURVEY 2000 follows dates throughout the flow of your programs. Every way through this process, SURVEY 2000 is recording where dates are used and where to locate programs and lines of code within all your programs. All of this information is pictured in a report that traces the flow of the date.

SURVEY 2000 is also capable of referencing redefines and data structures that are used in the application. Sometimes tools such as SURVEY 2000 provide too much information, which slows the programmers' progress in reviewing reports. However, SURVEY 2000 can be customized by programmers to include or exclude references.

Furthermore, programmers can limit the scope of the search from the complete system to a particular program or to a subprogram by changing switches in SURVEY 2000.

As a result of using SURVEY 2000, you will have a complete cross reference of every component of your system including data sets, source code, load modules, JCL, and CICS tables. Your staff need only review the results rather than spend countless hours manually sifting through all your source code and databases.

TRANSLATE 2000 is designed to automate file expansion, bridging, and code renovation. For each date format used throughout the systems, your programmers can specify in TRANSLATE 2000 a revised date format. TRANSLATE 2000 then performs a search and replace to update the date format in your files, programs, data elements, and even in copybooks.

SIMULATE 2000 simulates the date generated by the operating system. This enables your programmers to "reset" the systems date to any date, then run your systems to determine the effect the date has on their operations. The same process can be performed to the corrected system to test whether or not the problem is fixed.

The purpose of SIMULATE 2000 is to give your programmers the opportunity to test your system without fearing the changes in the system's date which could affect your production systems. The date maintained by the operating system never really changes to the test date when your programs use SIMULATE 2000.

Prince Software also has teams of technicians ready and willing to supplement you own technology staff. Prince Software has been providing such services for more than 20 years.

A Methodology

The struggle to define an enterprise-wide plan to address the potential hazards of the year 2000 problem is one that every company and government agency faces. Time is running out and the pressure of the immovable deadline can cause level heads to approach this problem illogically.

Your business can be faced with a double whammy: the year 2000 bug itself and the chaos that infects your staff as they try their old method of fixing serious problems—putting out fires. This technically will not work. The year 2000 problem is like a fire storm that is engulfing business after business. The local fire brigade may be no match for this bug. However, techniques exist that can be used to successfully combat the year 2000 bug.

In this chapter, we explore one such technique. There are many ways that your firm can approach the year 2000 problem. Many are offered by commercial services as discussed in the previous chapter.

There is no one solution that meets the needs of every business and government agency. The one presented in this chapter is simple enough that your own staff can use this as a model that can be easily modified to meet your organization's requirements.

The Process

Our model consists of five steps. These are:

1. The inventory process;

2. The assessment process;

3. The planning and repair process;

4. The testing process; and

5. The implementation process.

The inventory process is the starting point. Your year 2000 team searches throughout your firm for hardware and systems that keep your business operational. This process documents everything in your organization including the skills of your technical staff.

Once the inventory process is completed, the team can begin the assessment process. The assessment process carefully examines each piece of inventory to determine the effect the year 2000 bug has on it. This is also the stage where the team identifies what needs to be repaired and the priority of the repairs.

Next comes the planning and repair process. In some methodologies, these tasks are considered two separate processes. Our method combines these to suggest an almost seamless connection between these two activities since plans are adjusted while repairs are being made to the systems.

Planning is a vital component of the year 2000 solution. Repairs can be performed only if there are sufficient personnel and facilities to facilitate them. And since there is a limit to the amount of resources available for the project, traditional planning tools must be used to manage these resources properly.

Plans are used as guidelines for the technical staff to make your systems year 2000 compliant. Plans specifically list the tasks that must be performed to fix each system. Furthermore, plans list who must perform these tasks, the resources that are used to make the repair, and when those tasks are to be completed. The technical staff then works the plan to keep pace with the broader schedule of the year 2000 project.

After changes are made to your systems, the project enters the testing process. The testing process is designed to prove that the technical changes work. This is probably one of the most underrated aspect of any project.

The more testing that is undertaken, the better chance there is to discover problems with the systems. Catching these problems during the testing process enables your technical staff to correct the problem before the system is placed into production, where the problem could affect your operation.

Finally, there is the implementation process. The implementation process is the stage at which your fully tested system is moved into your firm's production environment. The "switches" are turned on and your revamped systems brings your company into the twenty-first century.

Throughout the rest of this chapter we explore the details of each of these processes. Each process encompasses many steps that must be performed in sequence to ensure complete results.

Inventory Process

The inventory process is the stage at which your year 2000 team surveys the computer assets of your organization. These assets include computer hardware, software, tools, technical staff, and all electronic devices that are used by your organization.

The inventory process is an information gathering task. Your team is required to prepare documentation about your firm's assets which will later be used to assess whether or not the asset is affected by the year 2000 bug.

It is critical at this stage of the year 2000 project that no one make any judgment as to the importance of the piece of inventory. When the piece is found, the staff immediately obtains critical information about it and records the information on the appropriate documents.

The Inventory Team

The makeup of the inventory team is crucial to the success of the inventory process. Team members do not have to have a technical background and in some cases a technical background can be a hindrance to the process.

Each inventory team member is given an inventory form which contains all the information that the team member must find out about a piece of inventory. The information itself is given to team members by your technical staff who are responsible for the piece of inventory.

Therefore, the skills required to become an inventory team member are not technical, although a technical background could help. The team member must be able to perform tedious, mundane tasks without an immediate sense of purpose. Their work will not be recognized for months and the final benefit of their work will not be realized for years.

The inventory team is the backbone of the entire project. Without competent results, the entire year 2000 project can falter—and you will not know about this until the first business day in the twenty-first century.

A good management approach is to reassign employees who are qualified to perform the inventory process to the year 2000 project team. Next, train them so that they can appreciate the importance of their new work and how their work directly affects the future performance of the firm.

Be sure to allow anyone who is reassigned the right to return to their previous assignment anytime during the inventory process. This serves two purposes. First, the team member knows that his or her job still exists. Inventory team members are typically concerned about job security. They usually do not mind helping in a crisis as long as they are not penalized.

The second benefit is that the quality of your inventory process falls dramatically once team members lose interest in the work. The company is better served if the team member returns to his or her regular job.

Another point that should be made during training is the opportunity for advancement that could accrue to a member of the team (or the lack thereof). Being selected for a special team gives employees a feeling of being recognized for having unique skills and possibly in line for advancement.

At the outset, set the record straight. Let all the employees—not only those who are selected for the team—know whether or not their instincts are correct. Be sure everyone has the same understanding. Otherwise, there could be a morale problem with your staff both during and after the year 2000 project.

Some staff members not selected for the inventory team will feel slighted and those who worked on the project will feel cheated if they are not rewarded—even if you did not promise to reward them.

Inventory Team Checklist

- Reassign detail-oriented employees to the team.

- Allow team members to rotate back to their regular positions.

- Be up-front with all employees on how team members were selected.

- Tell all employees whether or not being a member of the team is recognition of quality workmanship.

- Let all team members know if there is a reward for being on the team.

- Train team members on the technique of gathering inventory information.

- Monitor team member performance and do not hesitate to rotate them back to their regular jobs if the quality of work falls below acceptable levels.

The Inventory Database

At the center of the inventory process is the inventory database which is used to store information about each piece of inventory. You can purchase tools that include an inventory database or you can use tools you probably already have inhouse to create your own within a few hours.

The database should contain at least two tables: one table for software and hardware and the other for staff. These tables are not related to each other. Table 7.1 lists the information that should be contained in the software/hardware table for each item in your inventory database. Table 7.2

lists the information that should be contained in the staff table for each programmer on your staff.

Item name

Item description

Item function

Item serial number

Item model number

Item location

Level diagram number

Date item was acquired/created

Programmer who created the item

Manager responsible for the item

Manager's location

Manager's telephone number

Manager's beeper number

Manager's supervisor

Manager's supervisor's location

Manager's supervisor's telephone number

Manufacturer

Manufacturer's location

Manufacturer's telephone number

Vendor's name

Vendor's location

Vendor's telephone number

Purchased outright (y/n)

Licensed (y/n)

If licensed, date licensed

If licensed, date of renewal

Rights to change item (y/n)
Rights to show item with third party (y/n)
Rights to export item (y/n)
Is government approval required to export item (y/n)

Stand-alone item (y/n)
If not stand-alone system, then network ID

Incoming data feeds source
Incoming data feeds contact
Incoming data feeds location
Incoming data feeds telephone number
Incoming data feeds in year 2000 compliance (y/n)
Outgoing data feeds

Database dependencies
Index dependencies
Other system dependencies
Timing dependencies
Feed dependencies
Operating system settings and dependencies

Mission critical item (y/n)
Is item year 2000 compliant (y/n)
If not in compliance, priority number

Required tools (i.e., compiler)
Required libraries
Required languages
Required database management software
Required shared code

Executable location

Object module location

Source code location

Tools location

Library location

Shared code location

Database management software location

How many routines/screens/reports/databases/indexes must be brought into compliance?

The locations of these routines/screens/reports/databases/indexes

The solution for each routines/screens/reports/databases/indexes

Table 7.1 *Information that is contained in the software/hardware table of the inventory database.*

Most of the information required by the software/hardware table is self-explanatory. However, a few pieces of information need clarification. Each record in this table represents one piece of inventory called an *item*. This can be a complete system, a program, a computer, routers, calculators, components of your building security systems, elevators—the list is nearly endless.

Information described in Table 7.1 is not required for every record, only for those applicable items. It is safe to say that if the item is an elevator that you do not need to identify the locations of the source code of the software that runs the elevator. These may not be any available to your firm.

Also, some pieces of information such as incoming feeds and other dependencies are listed once in Table 7.1 although there are probably multiple feeds and dependencies. Each one should be identified. Therefore, the layout of this table and of the database will probably become more complex than the one shown in Table 7.1.

Each item must be assigned a leveling number. This is the item's number on the leveling diagram. As you recall from a previous chapter, a leveling diagram is a road map to your system. We speak more about a leveling diagram later in this chapter.

At the end of the inventory process, all the information applicable to an item must be entered into the database. This central depository of information becomes the foundation for the assessment process.

Employee name

Employee number

Date hired

Languages

Operating systems

Tools used

Interview done for each language/operating system/tool (y/n)

Table 7.2 Information that is contained in the staff table of the inventory database.

Like the information contained in the software/hardware table, information in the staff table (Table 7.2) is also self-explanatory. This information describes the skill set of your technical staff. This lists the computer languages that are known by each technician and the tools and operating systems in which they claim to be proficient.

Also note that each claim represented by the technician should be verified by a technician who is competent to give a technical interview. This means that when a technician is listed in the inventory database as knowing assembler language, then an interview has shown the technician to indeed be competent in that language.

A word of caution: Before asking your technical staff to list their technical skills, let them know that they will be required to pass a technical interview before they will be accredited with that skill. This disclaimer helps to cut down on the erroneous claims that normally are received in response to such a survey. Those technicians who have not used those skills professionally tend to back away from making claims that they later will have to prove.

Ask each technician to enter information directly into the table. You may consider creating a simple application to capture this information. You do not need to give each technician a technical review until after the assessment process is completed and you know the skill set that you require.

Inventory Database Checklist

- Create a database to store information about software, hardware, and technicians' skill sets.

- Each record containing software and hardware information must be related to the leveling diagram by leveling diagram number.

- Tell technicians to enter their skills sets directly into the database via a screen that you create.

- Tell technicians that they will be given technical interviews for every skill that they claim before being accredited with that skill in the database.

- Do not give any technical interviews until after the assessment process is completed.

Inventory Mapping

Besides gathering information about inventory and storing this data into an inventory database, the inventory process also requires that a map of the pieces of inventory be created. The map that is commonly used in complex projects is called the *leveling diagram*. As mentioned earlier in this book, a leveling diagram depicts the relationships among components of a complex project.

As the name implies, a leveling diagram has many levels of diagrams with each level going into greater detail than the previous level. Consider a company has many categories of systems:

- Accounting systems;

- Sales and marketing systems;

- Personnel systems;

- Legal services systems;

- Building services systems; and

- Computer operations systems.

Collectively all these categories are related to the higher level, general description of systems. However, beneath each category are other systems. The Accounting systems category might consist of accounts payable, accounts receivable, the general ledger, payroll, and bank reconciliation systems.

This relationship can be illustrated by using a series of leveling diagrams. The highest level diagram, as shown in Figure 7.1, gives a broad overview of all the systems in the firm. Each category of systems has its own lower level leveling diagram that shows the systems that compose the category. This is illustrated for the accounting category in Figure 7.2.

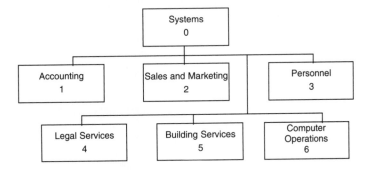

Figure 7.1 *The highest level leveling diagram that identifies all the categories of systems within the company.*

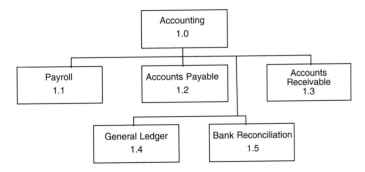

Figure 7.2 *The second-level leveling diagram that identifies all the systems in the accounting category.*

Each item shown on a level is assigned a number. In Figure 7.1, the category of Systems is assigned the number 0. The number 1 is assigned to the accounting category and other numbers are used for the other categories on the highest level leveling diagram.

The number assigned to an item on the highest level leveling diagram is then carried forward to the next level of leveling diagram. Notice that all the items in Figure 7.2, the next low-level diagram for the accounting category, are assigned numbers that start with 1. This number indicates the relationship to the item on the previous level.

Items on the second-level diagram (Figure 7.2) are also numbered consecutively beginning with zero. A period is used to separate the number used to relate the item to the previous level diagram from the item number of the current level diagram.

Figures 7.3 through 7.7 contain the second-level leveling diagram from each category of systems shown on the highest level leveling diagram (Figure 7.1).

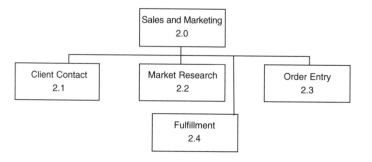

Figure 7.3 The second-level leveling diagram that identifies all the systems in the sales and marketing category.

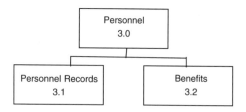

Figure 7.4 The second-level leveling diagram that identifies all the systems in the personnel category.

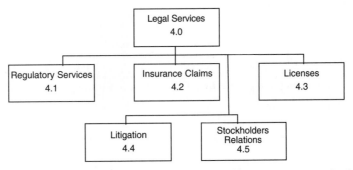

Figure 7.5 *The second-level leveling diagram that identifies all the systems in the legal services category.*

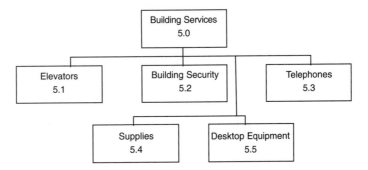

Figure 7.6 *The second-level leveling diagram that identifies all the systems in the building services category.*

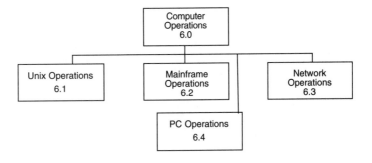

Figure 7.7 *The second-level leveling diagram that identifies all the systems in the computer operations category.*

Each system shown in the second-level leveling diagram has an associated level leveling diagram called the third level. The third level contains items that are components of the corresponding system and are typically program files and library files.

The program files contain the source code for each program while the library files contain common code. *Common code* is the term given to segments of code, sometimes called routines, functions, or procedures, that can be used by multiple program files.

A typical third level is shown in Figure 7.8. This leveling diagram depicts the programs and libraries that are used for the payroll system. Notice that the numbering sequence used in the first- and second-level leveling diagrams carries through to the third-level leveling diagram.

Each item on the third level begins with the number 1.1. This number shows the relationship the item has with the higher level leveling diagrams. Each of these numbers represents a level.

The number to the left of the first period (**1**.1.1) signifies the relationship to the first-level leveling diagram. The center number (1.**1**.1) indicates the item's relationship to the second-level leveling diagram. The number at far right (1.1.**1**) identifies the item on the third-level leveling diagram.

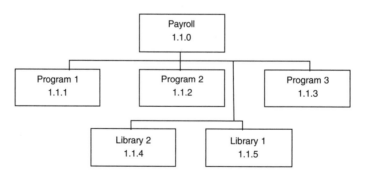

Figure 7.8 The third-level leveling diagram that identifies all the programs and libraries of the payroll system, which is under the accounting category.

Typically, leveling diagrams continue down to a fourth level which is shown in Figure 7.9. Here items that are directly related to Program 1 are identified and numbered. Notice that another number is placed to the right side of the previous item number. The complete set of numbers tells the genealogy of the item.

On figure 7.9, take a look at Date Routine 2, which is number 1.1.1.2. This number enables anyone to trace back through higher level leveling diagrams to learn the association of the item with all the other items in the firm's systems. Item 1.1.1.2 is a specific date routine that is used by Program 1 of the Payroll systems, which is in the accounting category of systems for the firm.

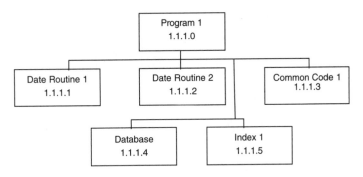

Figure 7.9 *The fourth-level leveling diagram that identifies all the date routines, common code routines, databases, and indexes used by Program 1 of the payroll system.*

A leveling diagram enables you to view systems of your firm at the complexity level required by a task. Say that you want to discuss the kinds of systems that must be addressed as part of the year 2000 project. You only need to look at the first level of the leveling diagram. You are not concerned about individual systems, programs, and date routines; therefore, there is no need to show this detail on the diagram.

However, you need this detail if you are assessing the impact of the year 2000 bug on the payroll system. The assessment of the payroll system requires the use of levels three and four of the leveling diagram.

Level three is used to identify all of the programs that are used in the payroll system. Level four of each of these programs is used to identify the items that must be reviewed or changed. You do not need to see the first and second levels of the leveling diagram because they do not provide you with sufficient information to perform the assessment.

The leveling diagram shown in Figure 7.1 is not complete. Items shown on the first level are typical but not inclusive of the categories of systems that exist in every firm. Likewise, a full leveling diagram contains second, third, and fourth levels for each item. This is omitted here due to space limitations.

You can use this leveling diagram as a model for your own. Modify as you require; however, be sure to maintain the proper numbering sequence otherwise the usefulness of the leveling diagram is lost.

Inventory Mapping Checklist

- Use a leveling diagram to identify inventory items and to show the relationship of each item to all of your firm's systems.

- Each level of a leveling diagram depicts greater detail for items that make up your systems.

- Relationships among items are identified by the leveling diagram number that is assigned to the item.

- A leveling diagram number is composed of sets of numbers. Each set represents the relationship the item has to a previous, higher level of the leveling diagram.

- Use only the appropriate level of the leveling diagram that shows just enough detail required to perform a task.

Inventory Tools

The inventory process is a tedious undertaking that requires patience and painstaking care. Otherwise, the information that is derived from the inventory process will be trash. You learned about tools in the previous chapter that automate the inventory process.

The reality is that tools automate parts of the inventory process, not the whole process. There are tools that explore programs and find date routines. Likewise, you can find tools that will identify all the programs, databases, tables, indexes, and libraries that are used by systems in your firm.

However, these automation tools probably will not help you inventory your building services systems such as building security and elevators. Nor are there tools that work in all computing environments. This means that the tool used to survey your MVS systems cannot be used on your personal computing systems.

Expect that you will need several tools to do the job and that each tool can report results in its own way. You can end up with a variation of the same report some of which may not be exactly the information that you require —and you cannot, in some cases, modify the report.

You must identify whether or not tools are available to automate the inventory process for all your systems. Do not assume that tools are available. If tools are not available, then your plans must be adjusted to reflect additional manpower needs to complete the inventory process.

Even if tools are available, a substantial manual process may still need to be performed. Keep in mind that the object of the inventory process is to produce two items: a leveling diagram, which is a road map to your inventory, and the inventory database that contains critical information about each item in inventory.

Tools that are employed during the inventory process probably will not automatically feed data into a leveling diagram or the inventory database. This means that someone must interpret information reported by the tool into data required by the leveling diagram and inventory database.

Tools require the use of resources. Identify those resources and other requirements at the beginning of the year 2000 project. This will give you time to provide training for your staff and reserve space on your computer hardware.

Before acquiring the tool, determine the run time for each system. How long does the tool take to inventory a typical system? The answer to this question helps you project the length of the inventory process and whether or not the tool can be used during your system's off-peak hours.

Most of all, avoid assuming that tools are the complete answer to your inventory process. Typically, this is not the case.

Inventory Tools Checklist
- Tools are unique to operating systems and platforms.
- More than one tool may be required to inventory your systems.

- Tools cannot inventory all your systems such as elevators and building security systems.

- Information generated by tools may need to be translated into data you require for your leveling diagram and inventory database.

- No tool automates the entire inventory process. Expect to perform a manual inventory in conjunction with the automated inventory process.

How to Inventory

To conduct an inventory, first develop the categories of systems that are used in your firm and plot them on the top-level leveling diagram as shown earlier in this chapter. This provides the framework for the next step in the inventory process.

Group your inventory team into subgroups, each of which is assigned a category of systems. It is the subgroup's responsibility to assemble the leveling diagram for their category. The number of subgroups will vary between firms. Smaller companies may have fewer subgroups, each being assigned to more than one category of systems.

Say that a subgroup is responsible for the accounting systems. This means they must inventory the payroll system, accounts payable, accounts receivable, general ledger, and bank reconciliation systems.

This can become a time-consuming venture. The length of time necessary to inventory each of these systems will vary. However, the time can be drastically reduced by having a subgroup assigned to each system rather than category of system. This is possible shortly after the inventory process begins when the second-level leveling diagram is constructed. At this time, you will have determined all the systems that exist under each category of systems.

Subgroups must inventory a system in a very methodical way. First, they complete all the levels of the leveling diagram. This serves as a road map for gathering information about each item on the leveling diagram.

Information must be immediately entered into the inventory database by the subgroup. Avoid the mistake of allowing the subgroup to write down the information on paper which is later transcribed to the database. This significantly increases the time required to collect the data and increases the opportunity for erroneous data being entered in the inventory database.

Each subgroup should be composed of a team leader, a person responsible for documentation (entering data into the inventory database and creating the leveling diagram), and the necessary technicians. The team leader and the documentation person should be comfortable with systems but do not need to be technicians.

Technicians will join and leave the subgroup as dictated by the skills required by the system at a given time. A Sybase technician, for example, is required only when the subgroup is inventorying a Sybase database. Until then, a Sybase technician is not required as a subgroup member.

Subgroup membership is fluid during the inventory process except for the team leader and the documentation person. These people should not leave the subgroup until a complete system is inventoried. And ideally when they leave, this two-person team would move to another system. The reason for this strategy is to ensure that continuity exists in inventory methodology and information gathering/reporting during the complete inventory process. Core subgroup members can make sure technicians elicit the proper information from the system.

Inventory Checklist

- Create highest level leveling diagrams first to depict categories of systems that need to be inventoried.

- Organize subgroups of the year 2000 team. The number of subgroups depends on the number of systems and time required to complete the inventory process.

- Assign each subgroup to a category of systems.

- Subgroups are responsible for creating lower level leveling diagrams and submitting information to the inventory database.

- Team leader and documentation personnel must remain with the subgroup throughout the inventory process. Technicians are assigned to the subgroup for as long as their skills are required.

. . . .

Assessment

Information collected during the inventory process is reviewed during the assessment process to determine which systems are affected by the year 2000 problem. Those that are not can be ignored by the year 2000 team. Those that are affected are examined more closely.

The assessment process must be just as formal as the inventory process. Potential trouble spots in the firm's systems must be clearly identified. Next, a determination must be made as to the potential damage the problem could cause on the firm's operation.

The assessment process also looks at the complexity of the problem. Is the problem with a routine written in code that can be easily fixed? Is the problem etched into a chip on the hardware that may not be fixable by the technical staff? Answers to these questions influence the time and resources that are required to rectify the problem.

In this section, we explore all the steps that are necessary to perform the assessment process for the year 2000 project. Keep in mind that many different methods can be used to assess the impact of the year 2000 problem on your firm.

Assessing a System

Begin the assessment process by referring to the highest leveling diagram. The leveling diagram is your guide through the systems of your firm. Your year 2000 team and their subgroups must conduct a systematic review of each category of system that appears on the first diagram.

Move down through successive levels until the detail level for an item is reached. Say that you start with the accounting systems, then follow through to the payroll system. You continue down to Program 1 of the payroll system, which leads you to Date Routine 1. This is illustrated in the leveling diagrams shown earlier in this chapter.

As you approach each level, you must ask questions that are relative to the system at that level. The first set of questions is raised at level 2 where you see all the systems that comprise a category of systems such as all the accounting systems (Figure 7.2).

Here are some questions to explore for each system:

- What is the event horizon?

- Does the event horizon extend beyond the year 2000?

- What is the impact to the firm when the system performs date calculations today for dates beyond the year 2000?

- Is the system required to stay government compliant? These are the systems that electronically file reports to government agencies and transfer funds such as those that are needed to pay payroll taxes.

- Is the system required to maintain basic operations? These are the systems that process orders, maintain payroll, send invoices, and send payments.

- Is the system required to maintain the books and records of the firm? These are the financial systems such as a budgeting system, asset management systems, and financial reporting systems.

Remember an event horizon is the date when the event (a system) begins to use dates in the year 2000. Some systems, such as those used by insurance companies, have passed their event horizon which means that erroneous dates are already being generated by those systems.

Furthermore, an assessment must be made to determine if your firm's operation will be hindered if the system misuses dates into the next century. In certain cases, there is no negative effect on your firm although there can be confusion about the century segment of the date.

Keep in mind that you do not have to determine if the year 2000 problem exists at this stage of the assessment process. You only need to determine the impact if the system is affected.

Once these questions are answered, you can assign the system a priority since you only want to concentrate efforts first on mission critical systems, then on systems that have the least impact on your firm's operation.

The payroll system would be a mission critical system for most firms. However, a system used to book conference rooms would have much less impact on the firm. Therefore, you could ignore the conference systems until the critical systems are fixed.

Assessing a System Checklist

- Systematically follow the leveling diagram during the assessment process.

- Determine the impact the year 2000 problem could have on each system.

- Do not determine if the system has the year 2000 problem until later in the assessment process.

- Assign each system a priority based on the negative impact the system would have on the firm if the system is affected by the year 2000 problem.

- Continue the assessment process based on the priority that you have given the system.

Assessing the Date Impact

The major focus of the assessment process centers around places in the system where dates are used for any purpose. You must look at each date routine and answer the question "Will this routine produce the correct date into the next century?"

The lowest level leveling diagrams, in concert with information in the inventory database, are used at this phase of the assessment process. Review the program level diagrams such as that shown in Figure 7.9 to identify the routines, databases, indexes, and other items that deal with dates. The location of these items can be found by reviewing the inventory database.

Here are typical dates used by various systems throughout a typical organization, making them likely targets for your assessment:

- Date hired;

- Birth date;

- Benefit enrollment date;

- Benefit eligibility date;

- Date assigned to a department;

- Date of next performance review; and

- Date terminated.

Examine the lines of codes where dates are used. If the code performs calculations, then simulate those calculations using the same operating system and platform as is used in production. This is important since the operating system and the platform can directly influence dates used by the code such as in the case where the program reads the systems date.

Test a series of dates both in the current century and in the twenty-first century. Also test the automatic transition to the next century. Many of these tests have been discussed in detail earlier in this book.

Avoid performing these date calculations by hand or on another computer. Chances are that the algorithm for the calculation is correct in the program. The problem could lie with how the date is handled on that particular computer. Also try not to make assumptions. Test every place a date is used in your systems, then make a judgment based on the results of the test.

Pay careful attention to date functions (procedures and subroutines). Typically, a call is made to a date function by code in the program. Sometimes information such as a date or a range of dates is passed, by the program, to the function.

Two problems could occur with date functions. First, the function may not accept a year 2000 date as a valid parameter. Simply said, the function will not recognize a parameter such as 12/12/2001. The function might accept 12/12/01. The 10-digit date causes the function to return an error.

The other problem is with the date calculated and returned to the program by the function. The results of such a calculation can be wrong. Therefore, you must carefully test all functions that use dates to determine if either problem exists with the function.

You must also assess whether or not the databases and indexes are affected by the year 2000 problem. As you have learned throughout this book, database fields may not be wide enough to handle the additional century digits. A quick review of the database directory will usually answer this question.

Likewise, indexes that are used to locate information quickly in a database must also be examined to determine if the key to the index contains dates. If so, an assessment must be made to decide if this date impacts the performance of the system.

Keep in mind that although a routine, database, or index uses a date, the date may not have an impact on your firm and changes might not be necessary. Consider an employee's birth date in your firm's personnel system. The date is probably in the mm/dd/yy format. Does the date really need to be changed to mm/dd/yyyy? Probably not, since this information rarely will ever be used in a date calculation. Furthermore, you can safely assume that the century is the twentieth century.

When you complete the assessment process, you will know if the system is affected by the year 2000 problem and specifically where in the system the problem lies. You need not be concerned, at this stage, about how to fix the problem. This will be investigated a little later in the project.

Be sure to update the inventory database with the additional information that you uncovered during the assessment process such as whether or not the system is in compliance. Not all the information about the system is elicited during the inventory process.

Assessing The Date Impact Checklist

- Review and test all places in the system that use dates to determine if the date is affected by the year 2000 problem.

- Perform all tests using the same or similar operating system and platform as is used in actual production.

- Do not make an assessment based on manual date calculations.

- Remember that some dates may not need to be in compliance although the century digits are missing from the date.

- Update the inventory database with information gathered from your assessment.

Assess Vendors and Their Systems

Special consideration must be given to systems that were supplied by outside vendors. Although you still follow the systematic analysis as outlined in the previous section, you must also assess other factors that can influence those systems.

First, determine if systems (or parts of systems) that are supplied by a vendor are affected by the year 2000 problem. If so, then you need to determine if those systems were purchased outright or licensed. Chances are that if you own the system, you have the right to upgrade the system if necessary and, therefore, you can treat the system as it were built inhouse.

A system that is licensed creates other potential problems. A further investigation is necessary. You must determine if the vendor is going to upgrade their system to become year 2000 compliant. Here are steps that you should take:

- Ask the vendor in writing whether their software is or will be year 2000 compliant by the beginning of 1998. Remember, you will need a year of parallel testing to make sure the fix works.

- Perform a complete credit check on the vendor and determine the vendor's financial status. You must be comfortable that the vendor has sufficient financial resources to finance the fix.

- Visit the vendor's site and see if the number of technical staff is sufficient to handle the changes while maintaining the current level of ongoing support.

- Ask the vendor in writing to see the plan and schedule for making the fix.

- Ask your staff who are in day-to-day contact with the vendor's first-line support staff if they have heard about any changes with the vendor.

You should not make any assumptions about a vendor, especially when the issue is one of whether or not your business can depend on the vendor to make their system year 2000 compliant. Make the vendor prove to you that the system will be in compliance well before the turn of the century.

Your assessment of the vendor should answer the question "Can and will the vendor fix the year 2000 problem in their system?" Notice that there are two factors that you must assess. The first is whether or not the vendor is in a position to correct the problem. Some vendors may not have the financial resources to undertake such a project, especially at no cost to their clients.

The second factor to determine is if the vendor is willing to make the repair. Some vendors may decide that the additional investment of capital into the product will never be recouped. Therefore, the vendor promises clients that the fix is forthcoming but in reality stalls until clients stops asking—or the deadline has passed and clients have taken evasive action.

Here are a few warning signs that might indicate you cannot depend on a vendor to bring the vendor's systems in compliance within the time frame that you require:

- The vendor refuses to respond in writing. This indicates that the vendor is not willing to legally commit to the fix in time. Do not accept any kind of response in place of one in writing.

- The vendor refuses to provide current financial statements certified by an outside auditor. The vendor may be hiding the fact that they are not in a financial position to fix their software.

- The vendor's site shows signs of fiscal problems. Clues include not enough desks, telephones, and computer equipment for the staff.

- The vendor's site shows staffing problems. Clues include more than enough desks, telephones, and computer equipment for the staff. Staff members are the first to realize that the vendor's business is in trouble and they are likely to move to other employment.

- The vendor does not have a plan or schedule in place to show you about how they plan to fix the problem.

- The vendor gradually becomes less responsive to your firm. Calls are not returned and personal contacts are avoided. The staff that normally handles your account no longer do so. This could be a sign that the vendor is about to go out of business.

Assessing Vendors and Their Systems Checklist

- Test vendors systems as if they were your own system.

- Determine if you have the right to change the vendor's system to bring the system into compliance.

- Study the vendor to determine if the vendor is actually upgrading the system for the year 2000.

- Do not assume that the vendor is truthful. Make the vendor provide you with facts that support every claim they make.

- Decide for yourself whether or not the vendor is capable and willing to fix the system without charge to your firm.

Perform Triage

After all the systems listed on the leveling diagram are assessed, you must perform triage. Triage, as discussed earlier in this book, is the medical technique used to quickly categorize a group of injured. In this case, the injured are the systems that your assessment process identified as being affected by the year 2000 problem.

The question that must be answered now is which systems get attention first. The answer depends on your assessment of the facts. You must divide the systems that need fixing into three groups:

- Systems that will survive without being fixed;

- Systems that will survive only if the system is fixed; and

- Systems that will not survive even if the system if fixed.

Those systems that will survive without being fixed include systems that are not affected by the year 2000 problem. These systems probably do not use any date data or, if dates are used, the system is already in compliance.

Also in this category are systems where dates are used and are not in compliance, but these dates do not have to be in compliance. Birth dates are a good example of this kind of date. Systems that use such dates practically are not affected by the bug and therefore should be placed in the nonfixed category.

The second group consists of those systems that must be fixed. These are the more obvious ones that stand out from the assessment process. They must be fixed before the turn of the century.

The last group is for systems that may have the year 2000 problem but are in such bad shape that they will not survive much longer, regardless of their status. Typically, these are legacy systems that have served the firm well and should be retired.

Systems in the second and third groups are the systems that need attention. Systems in the second group can probably be modified. However, systems in the third group must be rebuilt, purchased from a vendor, or trashed altogether.

Once the triage is completed, you need to prioritize the systems in each group based on the impact the system has on your firm should the system fail to become operational the first business day of the next century.

Triage Checklist

- Group all the systems that are affected with the year 2000 problem into the three triage groups: does not need fixing; needs fixing; and needs replacement.

- Systems with noncompliant dates may not need fixing if the dates do not materially affect the operation of the system.

- Prioritize systems in the second and third triage groups in the order in which they should receive attention.

Replace or Repair?

Another critical aspect of the assessment process is to decide whether or not the system should be modified or abandoned. This decision is based on a number of factors including:

- Age of the system;

- Future demands on the system;

- Complexity of the modification;

- Cost of the modification;

- Cost of replacing the system;

- Deadline for completing the modification;

- Missing source code;

- A vendor who decides not to make the system year 2000 compliant; and

- Legal entanglements that hinder fixing the problem yourself.

A system built on old technology might be difficult to repair economically. The code is probably in poor shape and technicians capable of fixing the system may no longer be readily available.

Furthermore, such legacy systems were built based on a business volume that is probably much lower than current volume. Your system is similar to a roadway handling 20 times more traffic than what it was designed to handle.

You can squeeze by another few years, but sometime soon you know the system will not meet the needs of your firm—and not because of the year 2000 problem. Maybe now is the time to bite the bullet and invest money in replacing the system. With the new technology and new tools on the market, you will probably spend less money to replace the system than you would pay to modify the current system. A careful technical and cost analysis of the system will determine which method is beneficial to your firm.

Replacing the system may not require a long lead time if you decide to purchase an existing system from a vendor. A cutting-edge system can quickly bring your firm into the twenty-first century within a few months. Many vendors will tailor their system to meet your firm's unique requirements.

Another place to look for a replacement system is with other firms in the industry. Some of your competitors might be willing to sell you a copy of their system as long as the system does not give either firm a competitive advantage. For example, a benefit system or a government compliance system could be acquired in this manner.

Replace Or Repair Checklist
- Evaluate every system that is not year 2000 compliant to determine if you should abandon or modify the system.
- Old legacy systems built on outdated technology are candidates for replacement.
- Purchasing a system from a vendor or from another firm in the industry is a fast method of replacing older systems.

Solutions

The final step in the assessment process is to decide how you are going to modify those systems that you determine need modifications. Solutions have been examined in detail in previous chapters, however, we will review them here. The basic solutions are to:

- Expand date fields in the database, then insert the century digits into the date.

- Change the code to include the century digits before performing date calculations.

- Create a sliding window where the system assumes the century based on the year. A 100-year sliding window could assume that years before 50 are in the twenty-first century and years after 49 in the twentieth century.

- Have technicians bit twiddle to squeeze a four-digit year into the same space used by a two-digit year.

- Use a bridge program to insert or remove century digits in data feeds between a year 2000 compliant system and one that is not in compliance.

Any one or a combination of these methods can solve the year 2000 problem with your system. The ideal solution is to change all the dates, and data that are derived from dates, to adjust for the century digits. This solution requires that all:

- Date fields be expanded by two digits;

- Programs that use date fields be adjusted to accommodate these two digits; and

- Date values stored in the date fields be converted to the four-digit year.

Many problems can prevent you from implementing the ideal solution. Here are other techniques on which you can fall back:

No Room to Expand All Date Fields

- Identify the date fields that are used as search criteria, sorts, and keys for index files, then expand those date fields and insert the two century digits.

- Dates that are used in calculations or in reports can be modified by code within the program without having to expand those fields in the database.

- Dates that are sent to other systems can be modified by using a bridge program.

- Dates that are received from other systems which are in the four-year digit format can be modified to a two-year digit format by a bridge program.

Out of Time to Make the Fix

- Create a sliding window by inserting a routine, similar to the one I have shown, into programs that access date data.

- Build bridge programs to send and receive data to and from other systems.

Solutions Checklist

- Select the most appropriate solution based on the time available to make the necessary changes.

- Be flexible with your solution. There is an ideal solution for every problem. However, the ideal solution may not be practical.

- Consider short-term solutions to meet impending deadlines that cannot be moved.

The Plan

A formal work plan must be created to ensure that all components of every system are repaired, tested, and placed into production. The year 2000 project is not like any project that your company nor your systems professionals have ever undertaken before.

The program has such grave consequences that you cannot permit your technical staff to approach this project in a haphazard way. Typically, your computer department loosely follows the prescribed method for developing a system. They sit with end users to understand the business needs. The technician's notes (a kind of functional specification) are translated into code, which is demonstrated to the end user and modified as necessary.

This works well for the average enhancement to the system, but falls short of being a complete work plan. Furthermore, this method is fraught with traps where problems can seep into the final version of the program. You cannot afford to expose the year 2000 project to this hazard.

From the onset, create a plan that addresses all the details of the project. The plan must answer the questions: "Who is doing what and when? " This simple question becomes very complex to answer.

First, you must use the results of the assessment process to plot all the tasks that are necessary to complete the year 2000 project. This information is entered into a project management tool such as Microsoft Project. There are many of these tools on the market. Each task must have:

- Start date;
- End date;
- Resources assigned to the task; and
- Dependencies.

A *resource* is anything that is needed to complete the task. This includes programmers, computers, disk space, tools, networks, and feeds to mention just a few items. *Dependencies* are tasks that must be completed before work can begin on the task.

Project management tools then produce various reports that help to keep everyone involved in the project focused on the tasks that need to be accomplished. There are work order reports that tell programmers what to work on. The programmer can then use the information developed in the inventory process and the assessment process to develop functional and technical specifications which are used as guidelines for completing the task.

The tool can also produce a critical path report which graphically shows the dependencies of tasks. This helps the project leader determine which task is falling behind and, therefore, requires reassignment of additional resources to the task.

Information can be updated in the project management tool. The tool can then be used to project the end date for the entire project. The projection is displayed in reports and on the screen in the form of a Gannt chart.

Gannt Chart

A Gannt chart is a graphic representation of all the tasks that are necessary to complete a project. Figure 7.12 illustrates a typical Gannt chart. This one is produced by Microsoft Project.

The left column is a listing of all the components of the first program in the payroll system. The first two lines, Payroll and Program 1, are not tasks. The rest of the items in the column are tasks. On the right margin of that column is a number followed by the letter d (i.e., 21d). This represents the number of days necessary to complete the task. Days when a programmer will be working on the tasks are plotted along the calendar. Notice that when the first task ends the second task begins. This is because these tasks are dependent on each other.

A critical report that is generated by the project management tool is the critical path of the project. This is based on the dependencies of each task. Figure 7.13 shows a typical critical path for the tasks shown in the Gannt chart in Figure 7.12.

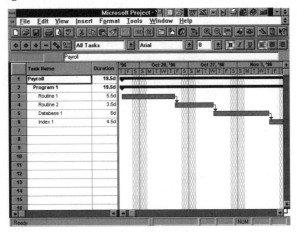

Figure 7.12 A typical Gannt chart for the payroll system. Tasks are listed in the left column and days when someone is working on the task are plotted on the chart.

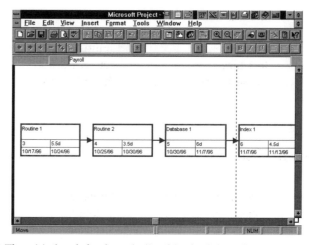

Figure 7.13 *The critical path for the tasks listed in the Gannt chart in Figure 7.12. All these tasks must be completed in order.*

Facilities

Plan to have the proper resources available in time to perform each task, otherwise the entire project can be unnecessarily delayed. Resources not only include staffing, talked about in previous chapters, but also items not normally associated with the year 2000 project.

Here are some resources that are commonly overlooked:

Desks, chairs, telephones, and computers;

- Floor space;

- Parking space;

- Support staff such as managers and personnel staff to handle the increased load; and

- General office supplies.

You can also use a project management tool to manage the process of acquiring these resources. For example, there is usually a three- to six-month lead time on acquiring new facilities. This becomes a task on the Gannt chart and becomes part of the critical path. That is, if the facilities are not ready in time, then the tasks of fixing the systems cannot be performed. As you can imagine, the project management tool is the perfect tool to keep your project on track and to determine the impact that missed deadlines have on the entire project.

Contingencies

What happens if the project falls so far behind schedule that the year 2000 comes and goes and your systems are still not in compliance? The planning process must include a contingency plan that can be implemented at the first sign that the year 2000 project is falling critically behind.

Here are a few ideas to consider when developing a contingency plan:

- Make arrangements with outside vendors who provide industry-wide computer services to let your firm run its data through their systems (i.e., payroll).

- Contact firms that offer services to handle orders over their telephones. This might be an alternative to your own order entry system.

- Determine if manual corrections can be made to data and reports until the fixes are completed.

Milestones

Create milestones for your year 2000 project. A milestone is a marker that indicates progress in completing the project. Milestones can actually be entered into the project management tool which, in turn, places the milestones in the appropriate place on the Gannt chart. Here are a few milestones that are commonly found in year 2000 projects:

- Find and locate each program within the system.

- Determine which programs require fixing.

- Determine which databases require fixing.

- Identify code or routines in each program that must be fixed.

- Correct the database.

- Correct code or routines in each program.

- Compile the new programs.

- Test the system.

- Complete preproduction requirements.

- Place the system in production.

The Testing

Every aspect of the year 2000 project must undergo complete testing. This includes unit tests by the programmer after changes have been made to each program.

A systems test comes next when all the programs, databases, indexes, and feeds are corrected. The systems test determines whether all the changes within a single system work well together.

Once the systems test is completed, the system is turned over to the quality assurance staff who continues the testing processing. Their function is to thoroughly test the system without influence from the programming staff. Part of their testing is a *soak test* whereby every variation of data in very high volume is processed through the system at normal speed. The objective of this test is to ensure that the system can withstand industry punishment.

The final test performed by quality assurance is a fully integrated test. This is where, when possible, the system is run in a pseudo-production environment to determine if the system has a negative effect on any other system in production. This test is the most difficult test to perform for two reasons: First, very few corporations have the resources to fully replicate the production environment. The other problem is that each system must be tested in a production environment with the other systems that have already been fixed. This means that a fully integrated system test requires all the systems to be repaired before the test can begin.

A further complication is that each time a problem is discovered and fixed, the full test procedure must be repeated. Traditionally this is not much of a problem because the test involves changes to one system at a time. However, most of the systems change in the year 2000 project and all of them must undergo testing at the same time.

Fortunately, there are tools that can help you with testing, as mentioned in the previous chapter.

Implementation

The final process in the year 2000 project is to place all the tested systems into the production environment, turn on the "switch," and pray that none of the system breaks down in production.

Moving all your systems into production is not an insignificant operation. This is time consuming and must be performed at a time when the current production systems are not operating. Some firms replicate the production hardware and the environment, then move the new systems into the replicated production environment. On a Friday evening, production is switched from the current production facilities to the replicated facilities. This technique is expensive but allows for an entire migration to occur with practically no impact to the production system. Furthermore, if the replicated production environment fails to perform correctly, the old production environment can be placed back on line relatively quickly .

Once all your systems are running in production, the year 2000 team must monitor the production closely for the next few months. Hopefully, if all goes well, your problems will be solved.

Happy New Year.

Index

Related Titles from AP PROFESSIONAL

Ordering Information

 **AP PROFESSIONAL**

An imprint of ACADEMIC PRESS
A division of HARCOURT BRACE & COMPANY

ORDERS (USA and Canada): 1-800-3131-APP or APP@ACAD.COM
AP Professional Orders: 6277 Sea Harbor Dr., Orlando, FL 32821-9816

Europe/Middle East/Africa: 0-11-44 (0) 181-300-3322
Orders: AP Professional 24-28 Oval Rd., London NW1 7DX

Japan/Korea: 03-3234-3911-5
Orders: Harcourt Brace Japan, Inc., Ichibancho Central Building 22-1, Ichibancho Chiyoda-Ku, Tokyo 102

Australia: 02-517-8999
Orders: Harcourt Brace & Co., Australia, Locked Bag 16, Marrickville, NSW 2204 Australia

Other International: (407) 345-3800
AP Professional Orders: 6277 Sea Harbor Dr., Orlando FL 32821-9816

Editorial: 1300 Boylston St., Chestnut Hill, MA 02167 (617) 232-0500

Web: http://www.apnet.com/approfessional